HOW TO CREATE AN INCOME FOR LIFE

Margaret Lomas

Wrightbooks

Also by Margaret Lomas

How to Maximise Your Property Portfolio
How to Make Your Money Last as Long as You Do
How to Invest in Managed Funds
The Truth About Positive Cash Flow Property

First published March 2002 by Wrightbooks
an imprint of John Wiley & Sons Australia, Ltd
42 McDougall Street, Milton, Qld 4064

Offices also in Sydney and Melbourne

Reprinted August 2002, September 2002, May 2003, August 2003 (with revisions), April 2004, March 2005 and March 2006 (with revisions)

Typeset in 11.5/12.6 pt AGaramond

© Margaret Lomas 2002, 2003, 2005, 2006

The moral rights of the author have been asserted.

National Library of Australia Cataloguing-in-Publication data

---

Lomas, Margaret.
How to create an income for life.

Includes index.
ISBN 0 7016 3651 3.

1. Finance, Personal. 2. Real estate investment. I. Title.
332.024

Cover design by Rob Cowpe

Printed in Australia by Griffin Press

10 9 8

Disclaimer
The material in this publication is of the nature of general comment only, and neither purports nor intends to be advice. Readers should not act on the basis of any matter in this publication without considering (and if appropriate, taking) professional advice with due regard to their own particular circumstances. The author and publisher expressly disclaim all and any liability to any person, whether a purchaser of this publication or not, in respect of anything and of the consequences of anything done or omitted to be done by any such person in reliance, whether whole or partial, upon the whole or any part of the contents of this publication.

Contents

Dedication

I never cease to wonder at the dedication, support and inspiration of my wonderful husband, Reuben.

You are not the wind beneath my wings—you are my wings.

Welcome to Your Future

I HAD A PHONE CALL from a client I have been assisting for many years now. She worked hard to pay down her first mortgage so that she could build her dream home. Having accomplished this a few years ago, she was now ready to buy her first property investment. When I explained to her that my heavy work schedule meant that I may have to bring in one of my very experienced staff to assist, she revealed that she was worried that there was no one else who knew quite as much as I did. "I only want to see you," she said to me.

When *How to Make Your Money Last as Long as You Do* was first published, it stirred up the 'negative gearing' industry. Since the mid-eighties, when the government first allowed investors to write off the losses incurred on a property investment against other income, people have turned to property as a viable investment. Subsequently, property developers and marketers began cashing in on the concept of 'buying a property for just $40 a week from your own pocket' as a way to attract people to buy their stock. It is only now, as some of those early investors begin to look at liquidating their investments, that they are realising this kind of investing may not have yielded such a good return after all. The $40 a week from an investor's own pocket, when considered in terms of its loss of value over time and the lost opportunity, is showing a very poor real return when compared to other investment vehicles.

How to Make Your Money Last as Long as You Do aimed to show people how negative gearing principles could be used to generate a higher than average return on property, provided the investor did the homework and chose property which I like to call 'positive cash flow' property—that is property which generated a profit from the first day, not months or years later.

For many years people have believed that the only way to gain a positive return from property was through 'positive gearing'. Yet, to achieve this an investor either had to be very lucky to find a property with a rent return which was considerably higher than average for its purchase price, or be fortunate enough to have substantial cash at the outset to minimise the borrowing costs and so produce a positive return.

How to Make Your Money Last as Long as You Do exploded this myth, and showed people how they could buy property without using any cash of their own and still get a positive cash flow from the first day. It motivated thousands of Australians to be more discerning in their choice of property investment, and once again guided people towards property. However, that book was only an introduction to the concept, and in many cases raised many more questions than could be answered in just one book.

So, when my client called and insisted on seeing only me, I knew this was because she felt that I was the one with all of the inside knowledge—information which she felt she needed in order to confidently embark on her investment plan. It was then that I knew I had to write another property investment book—one full of all of those little bits of information that I know about property and can share with others to help them crystallise their own investment plans.

Every day I receive email from people who have been caught with a property which either did not perform as expected or with net returns which did not even keep pace with inflation. These people enthusiastically embraced the concept of investing for their retirement, yet in many cases the experience has left them disillusioned, disheartened and with no real desire to attempt to invest further. Often the reason for the poor choice of property was the investors did no more research beyond the marketing material provided by the developer. They also may well have been swayed by emotions at the time. But, in many cases it has simply been a lack of knowledge from both the investors and the people advising.

It's no secret that the future of our middle-aged working population is in serious jeopardy. Our parents had large families, and my generation is now footing the welfare bill for the hundreds of thousands of aged pensioners, who insist on living well into their eighties! But, what will happen to us?

> ...there simply will not be enough money paid in taxes to provide pensions for us in retirement.

We chose to have smaller families, and the situation at present is that the only thing preventing a negative population growth in our country is immigration! It does not take Einstein to work out that there simply will not be enough money paid in taxes to provide pensions for us in retirement.

Sadly, our 'she'll be right mate' attitude is the very thing which keeps many heads in the sand, with the greater proportion of tax payers putting into place absolutely no plans for their own retirement. If you thought that living on $18,000 a year (the current aged pension for a couple) seemed impossible, then can you imagine what life would be like with nothing?

We must begin a plan for our own retirement, and we must start it today! If property is the vehicle that most attracts you, then this book will tell you everything you need to know to be sure that the property you choose has every chance for success. You will no longer have to rely on marketing material promising wonderful (and often unsustainable) returns, or the advice of well-meaning 'professionals' who really do not know much at all. You will have the knowledge you need. And, most importantly, you will learn that a property investment must be treated in the same way as any other investment; with a business brain, and not an emotional heart! Forget how you feel about the kitchen, the bathroom or the rose garden, and start looking at the returns and the potential of your investment.

By reading this book you receive access to free software which will help you do those very important figures which tell you just how viable an investment really is for your own personal circumstances.

So, don't wait another minute! Start reading and learning and taking responsibility for your own future. Realise that the biggest risk of all is the risk of doing nothing, and that retirement really can be a time of relaxation and fun, but it is all up to you!

Margaret Lomas
Glenning Valley, NSW
February 2002

1   To Invest or Not to Invest?

➠ **The time to take responsibility for your own future is *now*.**

➠ **Property is extremely low risk compared to other investments.**

➠ **You must have the right attitude before you can succeed.**

➠ **Do not rely on salespeople or developers for information.**

EVERYONE HAS HEARD the term 'great Aussie battler'. How many times have you seen a news report extolling the virtues of the latest lotto winner, a true 'battler' who has finally seen some luck?

We seem to revere the underdog, who proudly wears this badge as a testament to his Australian-ness. When this term was first used, it described those honourable people facing hardship after hardship; war, financial struggles and a host of other things over which they had no control. Through thick and thin they battled on, and so earned the title 'battler'.

Today, while we still have genuine cases of people facing sometimes unfair hardships, the term is much more loosely used, and seems to apply to anyone who gets through life on very little. In some of these cases, the reality is that having little is a result of inaction by the person—yet the ultimate reward is to join the elite ranks of the battlers!

Peter is a long time client of mine, and is a pretty good example of a battler. He came to me because a little voice inside his head spoke to him and told him that he should do *something*. I proposed a fairly simple starting point which reorganised his mortgage and provided a tight yet fair budget. Investing would come some time later. He wanted to think about this, and went away to do so (for a year!). During this time, he came across a property being offered by a local developer that he thought may have been a good opportunity for him. He actually got three-quarters of the way toward making this purchase, but in the end that same set of principles which was keeping him from getting ahead interfered and he withdrew! "We have our super," he said. When I explained to him that his superannuation was actually quite a small amount which would produce less than half of the minimum income he would need to survive, his answer was, "That's OK, we'll just drive around Australia in a caravan when we retire!" Very romantic but most impractical. I can see him driving this caravan at 60, but by 70 or 75 I really feel that he may be a little tired of touring!

> In the cases where there may be some risk involved, often the risk is so slim as to be negligible.

The truth is that Peter is like many other people—his fear of what may go wrong if he makes changes to his position and begins to invest outweighs his desire to provide for a comfortable future. His present reality feels comfortable enough (he is amongst the ranks of millions of other battlers, after all), but he cannot see how even this reality cannot be sustained once he reaches a time when he can no longer work.

What I do know about this kind of fear is this—it is simply False Expectations Appearing Real, which really means it is based on misinformation or lack of knowledge. In the cases where there may be some risk involved, often the risk is so slim as to be negligible.

The Point

Having purchased this book, you are one of the few people who has realised that it is time you began to take responsibility for your own future. This will mean that not only must you look at what you are achieving today, you must consider what you need to do to have a comfortable life tomorrow. This chapter will look at investing, and explore risk in real terms. It will also help you to identify when you will be in the best position to begin an investment portfolio of your own.

Risk

There is no question that all investing carries with it some risk. When we talk about risk, people automatically assume that this means 'losing everything', which is very often an unlikely possibility.

In financial terms, risk can be divided into three categories:

1. The chances of losing your money.

2. The extent to which returns may vary from expectations.

3. The safety of an investment vehicle in comparison to other vehicles.

Let's have a look at these risks as they apply to investing in property.

Chances of Losing Your Money

When investing in property, the most common thing people worry about is that they will lose everything. Since we usually do not use any of our own cash when we buy property, this can be translated into worrying that you will lose the house in which you live. Mostly, this is completely unfounded, providing that you do not become overexposed.

Here are two examples (please note that these examples do not include selling costs).

> Jill has a house in which she lives. It is worth $250,000, and she owes $120,000, so she owns $130,000 of this house. Her worry is that, if she invests in a property which does not work for her, she will lose her own home.

She buys an investment property for $140,000. This home costs her $146,000 to acquire, funds which she borrows from a bank.

She now owes a total of $266,000, and she has total securities of $390,000.

Jill did not do adequate research, and so did not buy a positive cash flow property. One year after her purchase, she finds that she can no longer afford the $65 a week she must pay out of her own pocket. In addition, she is not getting the rent she thought she would, and the house is vacant often. Because of the high weekly cost to her, she cannot afford to lower the rent to attract a longer term tenant as this would then cost her even more, so she is caught.

She decides to sell. Although property values have increased by 5% (making her investment property worth $147,000, and her own home worth $262,500), she wants a quick sale and agrees to take $135,000 for the investment property.

What is her position now?

- ⫸ She has a remaining balance on her mortgage of $131,000, as she did not get enough from the sale of the investment property to pay back all of the $146,000 she borrowed.

- ⫸ She has a home worth $262,500.

- ⫸ She owns $131,500 ($262,500 less $131,000).

- ⫸ She has a capital loss of $5,000 to carry forward and write off against any future capital gains (see Chapter 11 for more on capital losses)

- ⫸ She has also lost $3,380, which represents the input from her for 52 weeks at $65 a week.

As you can see her net position is not ideal, however it is also not too bad either. Certainly, she has suffered some loss but it is not nearly as drastic as total loss of her home. She is in a position where she is only slightly behind where she was, and she could once again recover her original position by trying again, with a positive cash flow property.

Jerry, on the other hand, is keen to get started. He owns an apartment in the city worth $230,000. When he purchased this, he borrowed 95% of the purchase price ($218,500), and funded the difference plus costs to the value of $22,000 from his savings. He owns $11,500 of this property.

Jerry has a further $20,000 saved. He wants to purchase another apartment as an investment, and chooses one with a value of $160,000. He borrows $152,000, and uses his cash to fund the difference plus costs, which is $20,000 altogether, as he has a high lender's mortgage insurance premium for borrowing more than 80% of the value of the property. His position is that he owns $19,500 of the two properties, despite having used $42,000 of his own money to buy them.

After one year, the properties have increased in value by 5%. The one he lives in is worth $241,500, while the one he rents out is worth $168,000. We will assume that his mortgage has not changed a great deal, as his investment is costing him $55 a week from his own pocket so he cannot afford extra repayments. He experiences the same problems as Jill, and is forced to sell. He takes $5,000 less than the value for a quick sale on the investment property.

His position is:

➠ He gets only $3,000 more for the property than he paid. He pays this amount into his personal mortgage, reducing it to $215,500.

- ➠ He has a home worth $241,500. He owns $26,000 of this property.

- ➠ He has lost $16,000 of his cash and can only write off $5,000 as a capital loss against future capital gains.

- ➠ He has also paid $2,860 to have the investment ($55 a week for 12 months).

The difference between the two is that Jerry, despite his enthusiasm, was not ready to buy. His risk was far greater than Jill's risk and his costs to buy were greater due to his need for mortgage insurance.

> When you buy positive cash flow property, you have room to move.

It is useful to note here, however, that neither Jill nor Jerry *lost* their homes, despite their investments performing poorly.

It is important to put this kind of risk into perspective in this way before you buy any property. And, as you will see in the coming chapters, even this risk can be largely managed if you choose only positive cash flow property.

The Extent to Which Returns Vary From Expectations

All too often the returns when we buy property are either misquoted by the agent or overstated by the developer in the marketing material. In addition to this, even where the expected rent return may be reasonable, it can be affected by the occupancy levels of the area.

When you buy positive cash flow property, you have room to move. As you will see in later chapters, positive cash flow property is an excellent choice if you wish to manage this kind of risk. Of course, careful research and asking the *right* kind of questions of the *right* people is just as important, and this will be covered in Chapter 6.

The Safety of an Investment Vehicle Compared to Others

The stock market crash in the 1920s brought devastation to hundreds of thousands of investors. People jumped off tall buildings, unable to face life any more as they saw their wealth disappear in a few short days.

In 2001, we saw the collapse of HIH, One-Tel and Ansett. This not only affected those people who had invested in these companies, but other smaller businesses such as suppliers, who were left with unpaid bills, forcing them into a financial ruin of their own.

When you buy property, you have no guarantee of success, but you always have the property. Have you ever heard of anyone waking up one morning to find that their property became worth nothing, overnight? I firmly believe that careful buying can even eliminate most of the cases where people have been caught with property for which they paid too much in the first place.

From this point of view, and as a comparison to other vehicles, property rates extremely low on the risk scale.

How do I know when I am ready to invest?

This is the sixty-four thousand dollar question, and, depending on who you ask, it comes with many different answers. As you can see from the examples, Jerry probably invested too soon. Jill, on the other hand, could have begun her investment portfolio many years earlier.

While when you invest is largely a personal choice, you must remember that there are many people who are not investing soon enough because they are being held back by ungrounded fears and a general reluctance to address their future. Some people do not even realise that they *can* invest! The following steps will help you determine your readiness to invest.

1. Your Attitude to Success

When you see someone getting ahead, what is your reaction? Do you think, "they are lucky, dishonest, always in the right place at the right time, or think they are better than everyone else"? If this is you, then you are never going to get ahead yourself, because you don't have the right attitude towards success. You are so concerned about where others are going that you haven't got the time to plan your own future. Realise that there are really very few examples of 'lucky breaks'—those people you see forging ahead are doing so under their own steam as a result of a lot of hard work and planning, and a preparedness to do what others won't!

2.   Your Attitude to Money

What are you like with money? Do you have unexpected expenses? Do you find that when you come into some extra money it seems to disappear and you are not sure where it goes? If this is you, the last thing you need is a positive cash flow property, as it will only give you even more money to waste.

> Budgeting does not always mean making cutbacks.

Whatever your income at present, you must learn to live *within* this income. And the only way to do this is to set, and religiously follow, a budget.

Budgeting does not always mean making cutbacks. What it does mean is always being sure that you spend 10% less than you earn. By doing this, you will be sure to always have the money you need, and you will be putting aside a little extra to allow you to invest sooner.

For some, the 10% may go to savings, while for others it may represent extra repayments into the mortgage. Either way, this is the first step of any investment plan.

I don't believe you should begin an investment plan until you are confident that you have formulated, and are sticking to, a budget. Once this is happening, you are ready to progress to the next step.

3.   Your Attitude to Risk

When you visit your financial planner, he or she will give you a 'risk profile' to complete. This will help to determine the areas in which you are most advised to invest. A high score will indicate that you can bear the highs and lows the sharemarket will bring, a middle score will see property and fixed-interest instruments recommended to you, while a low score will mean that cash management trusts and the like are the vehicles with which you will be most comfortable.

If you believe that property is for you, then you must assess your risk profile by answering the following questions:

a. Will I panic every time a tenant moves out?

b. Will a property market lull cause me to lose sleep?

c. Do I have to buy property in my own area so that I can keep an eye on it?

d. Am I unduly worried about tenant damage?

e. Does the thought of more debt make my heart race?

If you answer 'Yes' to any of these questions, then I would have to say you are not quite ready to invest in property. Work on those feelings and when you can say 'No' to all of the above then you can begin to look again.

If you are ready, then you must realise that even within a property portfolio, different types of property will carry different levels of risk. These will be outlined for you in Chapter 3.

4.   Your Assets

Your assets and liabilities position is very important—however almost every person I meet today is either not aware of, or overstates, his or her true position. It's not because they are not being truthful about what they own, it's more because people are confused about what an asset really is.

A *physical* asset is something you own which loses value over time or which produces no income for you. Cars, boats, furniture, pools, etc. are physical assets. In most cases, the family home is also a physical asset—it cannot produce an income for you unless you use it to leverage into other, income-producing assets.

Financial assets are things you own which produce an income for you, such as investments in business and equities products, investments in property, and investments in appreciating assets such as works of art, collectibles, etc.

For the purposes of determining if you are ready to invest in property, you can consider your family home but not any of the other investments mentioned above. Why is this? Because the family home is a *financial* asset to the bank (which will accept it as security for borrowings), and other appreciating assets or financial investments cannot be used as security.

5.   Am I Ready to Invest?

Make a list of the value of all of your property. Be realistic. Many times, when I ask a client, "How much is your house worth?", the response is, "Well I wouldn't take any less than $200,000 for it!" That was not the question I asked! When we think of the value of our house, we think emotionally.

Jack down the road may have his house on the market for $200,000, and you may feel that what you have is *at least* as good as Jack's house. The reality is Jack has not sold his house (so the price is notional value only), and you may be the only people who feel about your house the way you do! Others may not like it, and it may not be as saleable as you think.

When you consider the value of your property, think like a valuer does. Look at:

⮑ The number of rooms.

⮑ Recent sales in the area of an equivalent size.

⮑ The saleability of your home when compared to other sales in the area—poor, average, high.

Note that these things have little to do with how nice you have the house looking, or how much other people are asking for their properties. Cosmetic features of a house will add to saleability only, rarely to price. You may have spent $10,000 on a new paint job and a tidy up, but the price is unlikely to increase by more than a fraction of this expenditure.

Once you have this list, make a list of what you owe, or your liabilities. Here, you need to include any debts you have incurred on those physical assets. In fact, you must include all debt.

What is the difference between your assets (property only) and your liabilities? Depending on the overall value of your assets, you will need to have *at least* 30% of equity—that is your liabilities should not exceed 70% of your property value. Why is this? There are two reasons:

1. In order to avoid being in the position in which Jerry found himself, you must build in some leeway to stay on top. If you must sell a property quickly and at a loss, being sure you have the 30% equity to start with gives you some extra room to meet any shortfall and still have some equity in the property you still own.

> I like people to be able to invest without incurring lender's mortgage insurance...

2. I like people to be able to invest without incurring lender's mortgage insurance, as it is a very costly arrangement and usually means you start behind the eight ball, having paid out more to get your property. To do this, the total value of your debt cannot exceed 80% of your property. When you buy property, you can borrow the full purchase price *if* you have equity in property elsewhere.

In order to keep your total exposure below the 80% mark, you must start from a position where you have more than 20% equity, or owe less than 80%, and 70% is the general starting point. The following are two examples which may help you to understand this more fully.

Terry has a house worth $300,000. He owes $210,000 (70%).

The bank would let him borrow up to $240,000 against the house he has now, without the need for lender's mortgage insurance (80%). This means he would then have $30,000 left over to pay the deposit on another property (and meet the purchasing costs). If we assumed purchasing costs of, say, $6,000, this would mean that he has $24,000 left over as his deposit on the investment property.

In order to keep Terry exposed to no more than 80% of his total portfolio, he could buy a property for $120,000. His situation would then look like this:

Total property value: $420,000
                          ($300,000 + $120,000)

Borrowings: $210,000 (own home)
              $126,000 (investment, including costs)

Total borrowings: $336,000

Loan-to-valuation ratio: 80%

We have kept Terry exposed to only 80% of his total property holdings. As the values rise and he pays down debt, he will be in a position to invest again (see Chapter 5 for more information on this type of leveraging).

Rebecca owns a townhouse with a value of $150,000. She owes $105,000 (70%).

The bank would only allow her to borrow a maximum of $120,000 on this townhouse, without lender's mortgage insurance. This means she only has $15,000 to spend as a deposit, and if we assume purchasing costs at this level of $4,000, then she only has $11,000 as a deposit.

Her maximum purchase price to keep her liabilities at 80% of her assets would only be $55,000.

While it is possible to find properties at this price (and I have seen some with great cash flows and even have some listed on our Destiny Positive Cash Flow Property Register), she may be better to wait until she has, say, 40% equity.

While 30% equity is the rule of thumb, you can now see how this will be different with each person, and will be determined by the total value of the property already held.

My company, Destiny, offers free software available as a download, which includes a quick calculator for assessing your readiness to invest (see access details at the back of the book).

Conclusion

If you have made it through the five steps outlined, then you are truly ready to begin your property portfolio. There is much to learn, and the rest of this book will provide you with an abundance of information, all equally important to your success in investing. You will no longer need to rely on the information provided by salespeople and developers—you will develop the ability to ask the right questions and give yourself every possible chance of success. Read on!

2 What is Positive Cash Flow Property?

➠ **Positive cash flow property is different from positive gearing.**

➠ **Buying an investment property is a business decision.**

➠ **When you buy positive cash flow property, the number of properties you can buy will technically be unlimited.**

PEOPLE ASK ME EVERY day to share with them the 'secrets of wealth', as if there were a magic spell that could be cast upon them which would instantly turn them into millionaires. I have met people who have spent upwards of $20,000 attending four-day seminars designed to provide them with a pathway to an '$80 million property portfolio' in a few short years. Generally they find the strategies are dubious at best, tread a very fine legal line and are definitely not for the faint-hearted. Usually there is more money to spend before the full deal is revealed, and by this time the person is somewhat disappointed and realises that there is no real get-rich-quick scheme.

So, once and for all, let me spoil the fun and reveal the secret! If you want to be wealthy then you must somehow create an income which continues to be paid to you long after you choose to stop working, an income which requires no personal exertion—we call this *passive income*. A high-paying job is very nice and will allow us to live a lavish lifestyle today, and an expensive house and car will certainly give us the outward appearance of wealth. Yet, when the income stops these luxury items will provide no support to us in the way that a passive income can.

Consider Frank Lowy, the man who started Westfield. If he chooses to spend a day in bed or at the beach, does this give all of those tenants in Westfield shopping centres a day off from paying the rent? Of course not! Unlike the income you most probably earn, his income is not dependent on any effort which he must personally exert on a daily basis.

Think about your own income. When you turn 60, and you are feeling somewhat tired (after 40 years of employment), will you be able to just stop? Assuming there is a pension at all, it is likely to be approximately one-third of your final year's salary (around $18,000, for a couple). Imagine that! Even without a mortgage to pay, do you think you could survive on this small amount? It's no wonder so many of our aged population have 'too much week left at the end of their money'! I have many relatives in exactly this position—people who enjoyed successful working lives filled with fun and travel, now budgeting to simply survive. At a time when most of us hope to be enjoying the best years of our lives the majority of us will be living a reality far from this.

> It's no wonder so many of our aged population have 'too much week left at the end of their money!'

The Point

The time to address this problem is now. And the way to address this problem is by commencing an investment portfolio which will ultimately provide the passive income you will need to create an income for life. This chapter will introduce you to the concept of positive cash flow property, so that you can better understand the most effective way to invest in property.

WHAT IS POSITIVE CASH FLOW PROPERTY?

When I try to explain this concept to people, few really grasp it on the first, or even second, attempt. I was surprised to find readers of my first book phoning to talk to me about 'positive gearing', despite the fact that the book had tried to make the distinction between this and positive cash flow property.

The best way to explain positive cash flow is by first looking at an alternative concept which most people *do* understand—that is, negative gearing.

How Does Negative Gearing Work?

Negative gearing is the term used to describe the process of writing off the losses incurred on a tax-office-approved investment against other earned income, resulting in less tax being paid, or a tax refund. In the case of property, it is when the income on a property (the rent) is not enough to cover the expenses, and you *lose* money. Since property is a tax-office-approved investment (if it meets the criteria below), purchasers of property where the purpose is to produce an income are able to claim a tax deduction for any expenses incurred which exceed the income made by that property.

To qualify as an approved investment, the property must:

- Be income-producing or become so within 12 months of the purchase.
- Not be vacant land (unless it is to be developed within 12 months).

To understand how the process for investing in negatively geared property works, let us look at an example.

Michelle and Geoff have been advised by their accountant to look at buying an investment property as they pay too much tax. What the accountant really means is that, at present, Geoff, who earns wages, has no real access to any tax deductions. So, they find a nice house down the road. They have lived in the area for 15 years and want to invest here for their future. The price is $140,000, and the expected rental return is $140 per week. The house was built in 1980.

Since they have considerable equity in their own home (see Chapter 9 for more on borrowing), they can borrow the full purchase price, plus all of the costs, which are shown on the following page.

Purchase stamp duty (NSW)	$3,390
Conveyancing and searches, etc. (approx.)	$1,500
Loan application	$700
Loan stamp duty (approx.)	$525
Total costs to purchase	**$146,115**

If we were to assume interest on the loan of 6.25%, let's have a look at the income expense position of this new property.

Income*		Expense	
Rent	$7,000	Rates	$1,200
		Repairs (approx. p.a.)	$1,000
		Bank interest	$9,132
		Management fees	$713
Total yearly income $7,000		**Total yearly costs**	**$12,045**

*50 weeks per year occupancy

Before tax breaks, it looks like Michelle and Geoff may be set to lose quite a lot of money. However, as the government allows them to offset this loss against other income, the position can be slightly improved by applying for a deduction on the income tax to be paid.

Geoff earns $50,000 a year, and Michelle earns $10,000. As you will see later in this book (Chapter 11), a situation like this may best be served by buying the property in Geoff's name only. At present, Geoff pays $11,772 in tax, giving him a net take-home weekly pay of $735.15. Assuming the property is purchased in Geoff's name only, then Geoff's position after buying the property looks like this:

Income from his job	$50,000
Rental income from house	$7,000
Total income	**$57,000**

Property costs	$12,045
For calculating tax	
Geoff's new taxable income	$44,955
(gross income less property costs)	
New tax	**$9,658**
For calculating cash in hand	
Total income earned	$57,000
Less expenses of the property	$12,045
Less new tax	$9,658
New cash in hand	**$35,297**
	($678.78 a week)

From this table you can see:

- Geoff has a lower taxable income even though he earned $7,000 (gross) more from the property.

- Geoff initially pays out $5,045 more than he earns from the property.

- Geoff pays $1,514 less to the tax department.

As a net figure, this means that he pays out $2,931.24 for the property, or $56 a week, which comes from his own pocket.

Note that before the property purchase Geoff had $746.69 a week as a disposable income, and after the purchase he has only $678.78. In simple terms, this means that he is losing money every week. Each week, Geoff pays out of his own pocket to provide a home for someone else!

> Each week, Geoff pays out of his own pocket to provide a home for someone else!

I can hear you all saying, "Why would he do that?", and I have to agree, it does seem like a little bit of madness. I have seen people paying out much more than this amount, every week, because their accountant has advised them that they need a tax deduction! However, there is some method in this madness—Geoff and Michelle have invested in the hope that the ultimate growth in their investment will outstrip the value of the $56 per week. There are, however, some problems with this.

What is the Real Extent of the Gain?

Let's project ahead five years. We will assume that during this time, the loan has remained interest-only while Geoff and Michelle continue to pay off their own home (see Chapter 11 for more information on loan structuring), and the interest rates have not changed over time.

The property has appreciated at 5% per year (this is a reasonable average, slightly above inflation rates, which for this example will be 3%). At the end of the fifth year, the value of the property is $178,600. As they financed the entire purchase price plus costs, their 'investment' is limited to any negative cash flow, or the money they paid from their own pocket. Let's assume at this point they decide to sell the investment property.

> Michelle and Geoff have put in a total of $15,608 ($2,931 per year indexed to inflation), which is their after-tax commitment. You can see that the original $14,655 is now worth more as the time value of money decreases its purchasing power. (To give you an idea of how this works, $1.00 in 1966 was worth 11¢ in 1999!)

Let's look at the final figures:

Sale price	$178,600
Purchase price	$140,000
Gross profit	**$38,600**
Less: Costs to buy	$6,115
Costs to sell (approx. legals)	*$2,000*
(approx. agent's fees)	*$6,000*
Costs to maintain	$15,608
Net to Geoff and Michelle	**$8,877**
Return on investment: 6.34% or 1.26% per annum (gross)	

This is not a great return, and you would be much better off to simply invest in a cash management trust or in government bonds, where you have an almost 100% guarantee of at least a return of your capital!

But there is one more thing we need to consider, and that is capital gains tax.

Under the Ralph regime, any property purchased after 21 September, 1999 and subsequently sold would be liable to capital gains tax if a gain were made. For investments held 12 months or more, this tax is discounted and so levied on just half of the net gain at the taxpayer's top marginal rate of tax (that is, gain after purchasing and selling costs divided by two).

In Michelle and Geoff's case, their taxable gain would be $12,242. If we assume that they dispose of this property while Geoff is still working, then he will incur capital gains tax of $3,581. This now means that, in addition to losing money *every* year (a total of $15,608), they lose another $3,581 at the point of sale (see Chapter 10 for more information on capital gains tax). This has reduced the actual gain to just $5,296.

And, what if the return on the property does not sit at a nice average 5%? We can never know just how a property is going to perform from a capital growth point of view, and therefore should never buy property based on a desire to see a strong capital gain to the exclusion of other factors, such as cash flow.

What was the Real Motivation for Buying the Property?

You will hear me repeat many times throughout this book that the reason we should buy property is to produce a passive income, not a short- or medium-term return by turning over the investment. In the example of Michelle and Geoff, they made two major mistakes—they bought a property because they wanted a tax deduction *and* they sold it to try to make a profit on the purchase price (a capital gain). They are now in a position where they have no more money than they could have had if they had chosen another, equally secure vehicle (this is not to say that property is not safe, as you will see), they have probably had the usual 'landlord' headaches (covered later in this book), and they have just sold their potential passive income, meaning that any retirement income they had hoped for from this investment is now gone.

What was the Opportunity Cost?

By spending that money ($2,931 per year) on this property (which remember, is a loss) they have actually also lost the opportunity to do something more profitable with these funds—such as make extra repayments into their current personal mortgage, investment into other vehicles or, more importantly, perhaps make extra repayments on a positive cash flow property! Read on to find out more about what this really means.

POSITIVE GEARING

If negative gearing means that you lose money, every week, then positive gearing has to mean that you make money every week. This sounds wonderful! So why doesn't everyone do it? Because, like all good things, its just not that easy.

How Does it Work?

Positive gearing is when the income you make on a property is more than you need to pay the expenses, and you win! And, so does the tax department, because it will tax you on the gain. This is not so bad, really—we live in a beautiful country and someone has to pay the taxes to keep it that way. However, there are only two ways that you can get a positively geared property, and neither of them are easy to achieve.

High Rent Return

The first method is to find a property which has a higher than usual rent return for the price you are paying. As a rule of thumb, a property will usually return 0.10% to 0.11% of its purchase price as a weekly return. So, a $200,000 property will probably give you $200 to $220 a week. If you can find a property returning at least 0.175% of its purchase price (in the case of a $200,000 property, this would be $350 a week), then there is a good chance

> You are not buying to make a short- or medium-term gain. You are buying to get a passive income...

that it may return an income greater than its expenses. This can be done—but rarely in capital cities. A reader once asked me, "How do I find a positively geared property in Melbourne?" My response? "You don't!", and the same can be said, in general, for all capital cities. To find a property like this you may need to go out into the lesser populated areas in each state.

Now, I can hear some gasps of horror—"But what about capital growth? You won't get any away from the capital cities." You may be partially correct, as some areas out of capital cities are not usually exposed to huge capital growth. But so what? You are not buying to make a short- or medium-term gain. You are buying to get a passive income, and, just as long as the property satisfies a host of other criteria, which will be outlined later in the book, then you will be ahead.

Here's an example:

> Sally and Dean find a town in NSW which has a population of 50,000. Housing prices are quite low but properties for rent are becoming a little scarce. They find a townhouse, with a purchase price of $115,000. The rental return is expected to be $210 a week.

They have some equity in their own home so they borrow all of the purchase price, plus costs, which are:

Purchase stamp duty (NSW)	$2,515
Conveyancing and searches, etc. (approx.)	$1,500
Loan application	$700
Loan stamp duty (approx.)	$500
Total costs for the purchase	**$120,215**

Assuming that interest on the loan is 6.25%, the income expense position of this new property is shown opposite.

Income*			
Rent	10,500	Rates (country town)	$1,000
		Repairs (approx. p.a.)	$500
		Body corporate	$400
		Bank interest	$7,513
		Management fees	$945
Total yearly income	**$10,500**	**Total yearly costs**	**$10,358**

*50 weeks per year occupancy

Before tax, Sally and Dean will make $142 a year. They will be taxed on this at their current marginal rate of tax, which is 30%, meaning they have a net gain for the year of $99, or about $2 a week. Not much, I must say, but this will only be the start. As you will see later, there are things which can be done to bring this property into a more profitable position fairly quickly.

Cash Deposit

The second way to purchase a positively geared property is to contribute a deposit in cash. Many of my clients seek advice as to whether they should use cash they have saved or otherwise acquired to buy an investment property. The following example will help you see why I give the answer in the way that I do.

Beryl has received $70,000 as an inheritance. She decides to use it to buy an apartment in the city as an investment. She finds just what she's looking for at a price of $160,000. The return is $180 a week. She funds this purchase using the $70,000 and an interest-only loan from the bank.

Beryl's costs are:

Purchase stamp duty (NSW)	$3,740
Conveyancing and searches, etc. (approx.)	$1,500

Loan application	$700
Loan stamp duty (approx.)	$450
Total costs to purchase	**$166,390**
Total loan required	**$96,390**

Assuming interest on the loan of 6.25% the income and expense position of this new property is as follows:

Income*		Expense	
Rent	$9,000	*Rates*	$1,200
		Repairs (approx. p.a.)	$500
		Body corporate	$400
		Bank interest	$6,024
		Management fees	$788
Total yearly income	**$9,000**	**Total yearly costs**	**$8,912**

*50 weeks per year occupancy

> **Beryl...has received a return of $62 a year for her investment of $70,000!**

Beryl's gross position is that she has $88 a year before tax. At the 30% tax rate, this will be reduced to $62. Still a positive cash flow but let's look a little closer! In reality, since Beryl does not plan to sell this property to realise any capital gain, she has received a return of $62 a year for her investment of $70,000! Considering this, what do you think my answer would be to someone asking whether to use cash to buy an investment property? If your aim is to buy a property which you intend to keep, the answer is a resounding *no*! I would be far more inclined to place the $70,000 into a well-balanced managed fund (or several) and borrow the entire purchase price for the property, if this is at all possible (Beryl would need property equity elsewhere to achieve this).

THE BEST TILL LAST!

In fact, I do not recommend either of the above. I am an experienced property investor and I have made some mistakes of my own in the past. These mistakes have taught me so much, and more importantly led me to seek out and understand the true meaning of 'positive cash flow property'.

I have been very encouraged over the past year to see people from all walks of life willing to take the plunge and begin their own property portfolio. I am, however, still seeing people fall into two major traps in how they think:

1. *Cars, boats, furniture, etc. are assets.* These are *not* assets as they hold little second-hand value and cannot be used to leverage into other, income-producing assets. Even the family home is not an asset until you use it to buy other assets—in fact it will be your biggest liability, as it will cost you money for the rest of your life and never return an income to you.

2. *Property is purchased with 'gut instinct'.* I had a client call me once to tell me that he was buying a property in Bondi. "Why are you buying it?" I asked. "Because it is in Bondi," was the response. "Does it have a positive cash flow?" I asked. "No, but it is in Bondi!" He could not understand why I was not impressed by this. He went on to explain how the capital growth would be huge and how it had great views! Now, had he wanted to live there then perhaps I would have been more enthused. But he had the wrong reasons for wanting this property. He cannot know what the capital gain will be like, and, just in case you missed it before, he should never want to sell the property as then his retirement income from this investment will be lost. The important questions, like occupancy rates, other developments in the area, liquidity and so much more all went unanswered as the emotions of purchasing in the famed 'Bondi' took over.

Use Your Business Head!

Buying property is a business transaction, even where the property is residential. And like all business transactions, it should be done with a business head and never on the emotion of the moment. Knowing whether a property is positive cash flow is the first step in a string of important steps when buying property. When I look at property, if the cash flow is not positive, then I go no further on that property. It's very simple!

How Does it Work?

Positive cash flow can occur on a property where the loss is largely on paper. A property with a large enough on-paper deduction can even take a loss and push it into a profit! Until now, we have looked at examples where property has been bought which carries deductions only on the expenses. While this is the case, you will need to search far and wide to find property where the rent return is high enough to meet the expenses.

> Positive cash flow can occur on a property where the loss is largely on paper.

In September 1985, the government introduced new rules for people wishing to purchase property as an investment (see Chapter 10 for more information on tax). In a nutshell, the new rules mean that an investor can now write off the costs of the construction (even where they did not construct the property themselves), as well as any furniture, fixtures and fittings associated with the property, at rates set by the tax department. These items are 'on paper' only—in other words, you get tax back on items to which you do not have a continuing commitment—money back, without paying money out.

Whether a property has a positive cash flow or not will depend on many things, such as the income, the rate of interest on your loan, the deductions allowable and your own personal rate of tax. A property creating a positive cash flow for Mary may not do so for Jake if they are in different tax brackets.

As you are by now probably thoroughly confused, let's have a look at an example of positive cash flow property.

Mark buys a new property, which was constructed in 2002. He pays $220,000 for this property and expects a rent return of $245 a week (it is furnished and should get a little more than average). The cost to build this house was $160,000. When it was built, it had fixtures and fittings to the value of $10,000, and furniture to the value of $12,000.

As it was built after 1987, Mark can claim construction depreciation (known as 'capital works deductions') for 40 years at 2.5%, and his fixtures, fittings and furniture also carry deductions at various rates (see Chapter 10) over time periods from one year to twenty years. He can also claim his borrowing costs over five years. For this example, let's say that he has fixtures, fittings and furniture depreciation in year one totaling $10,000 and borrowing costs of $1,500. He borrows the entire purchase price plus costs, which are:

Purchase stamp duty (NSW)	$6,190
Conveyancing and searches, etc. (approx.)	$1,500
Loan application	$1,500
Loan stamp duty (approx.)	$900
Total costs to purchase	**$230,090**

With interest on the loan of 6.25%, his income expense position looks like this:

Income*		Expense	
Rent	$12,250	Rates	$1,200
		Repairs (approx. p.a.)	$500
		Bank interest	$14,380
		Management fees	$1,103
Total yearly income	**$12,250**	**Total yearly costs**	**$17,183**

*50 weeks per year occupancy

It would appear that this is going to be a very expensive exercise for Mark, as the loss at this stage is $4,933, or $94 a week. But wait! Remember the depreciation? What effect will that have for Mark?

At the present moment, Mark earns $50,000 per annum, and brings home $735 a week. Let's look at what this purchase will do for him.

Income from his job	$50,000
Rental income from house	$12,250
Total income	**$62,250**
Property costs	$17,183
Other depreciation deductions (2.5% construction, $10,000 other, plus loan establishment costs $300)	$14,300
For calculating tax	
Mark's new taxable income (gross income less property costs and deductions)	$30,767
New tax	**$5,402**
For calculating cash in hand	
Total income earned (wages plus rent)	$62,250
Less expenses of the property	$17,183
Less new tax	$5,402
New cash in hand	**$39,665** ($763 week)

We can see from this that the on-paper deductions have not only wiped out the $94 loss, they have allowed Mark to obtain a profit of $28 a week after tax! That is, $28 a week more than he was earning before he bought his property. This is money to put into his own pocket, or more importantly into the mortgage and so accelerate the repayments and the rate at which he owns the property! It is very important to note here that this property is *not* positively geared as the $28 extra which Mark earns is not subject to tax. Why? Because it is the *after-tax* amount. In fact, the $28 is part of the tax which he got back as a refund (or elected not to pay at all through a tax variation request—see Chapter 10).

> There are many advantages to investing in positive cash flow property...

When you see examples like this, which I can assure you are most possible, then it truly makes you wonder why someone would in fact buy property which costs $40 a week from their own pocket.

There are many advantages to investing in positive cash flow property, over and above the obvious one of not having to put your hand in your own pocket and so lose precious money which you may need for other things. These advantages will be covered in depth in later chapters, along with techniques for maximising your investment into property and leveraging to increase your net worth.

One Clear Advantage

Let's have a look at a small problem which Michelle and Geoff may face when they decide they would like to expand their portfolio and invest further.

At present, they have committed $68 a week to their investment. They are managing this comfortably from their surplus funds, after having met all personal and household expenses.

As the value increases across the two properties (their home and their investment), they may want to invest again. But, how many lots of $68 a week can they afford?

When you negatively gear property, you are limited in the number of properties you can purchase by your surplus income. It may be that Geoff and Michelle can only afford one more, regardless of how much equity they manage to get through increasing values.

However, when you buy positive cash flow property, the number of properties you can buy will technically be unlimited. At the very least, it will only be limited by your equity, which will increase at a faster and faster rate as you add more property to your portfolio!

Wonderful, isn't it?

Conclusion

A gentleman once approached me at an expo. We spoke for some time about his love for property and his success (not always orchestrated) so far. In conclusion, he made an interesting comment. He said, "When I invest in property, I am the master of my own destiny. I know it will always have some value, because property always does, and I never have to worry about someone else making a decision which ultimately results in me losing, as in the case of HIH and One-Tel."

He had a good point. If you add to this thought careful research and being sure that your chosen property has a positive cash flow, then you could do a lot worse as an investment. I would venture to say that property may well outclass many other possible choices.

3 What Are My Choices With Property?

➠ **Property comes in many shapes, sizes and areas.**

➠ **Diversification can simply involve having many different *types* of property in different *areas* within your portfolio.**

➠ **All of the property types outlined in this chapter offer viable opportunities to investors who are prepared to do the research.**

I AM A FINANCIAL ADVISER so, of course, I am well aware of the benefits of having a balanced portfolio. I have been to enough lectures and seminars to know just how to put together a portfolio which has a balance across many asset classes. Yet still I feel an inner turmoil when I think of this concept in terms of the people who have asked for my help in the past.

In financial advising terms, a balanced portfolio involves choosing investments from fixed interest, property, shares and cash. For some people, a portfolio such as this would mean that they would spend most of the time worrying about 80% of their portfolio. By encouraging these people to spread their investing, we would in fact be suggesting that they invest in areas with which they have never been truly comfortable.

Investing is a truly personal thing. I have a client who owns 11 properties. He has no other investments. Is he worried by this? Not at all! He loves his property and it is providing a great income for him. When I asked him why he had no shares he gave me a horrified look and said, "Are you kidding? I'd never get any sleep!" The point here of course is that, while experienced investors should at some time look at hedging their bets by diversifying into other classes, if to do so would mean that they would be pushed too far out of their comfort zone then it is probably not such a good idea at all.

> People choose property because it has a proven element of safety...

People choose property because it has a proven element of safety with a good rate of return. They like property because they understand it and feel as if they have some control. And, if you are one of these people, then this does not mean you cannot diversify your portfolio. For you, diversification will simply involve having many different *types* of property in different *areas* within your portfolio.

The Point

When people think of property as an investment, they automatically reach for the local realtor and look at what is in their area. Property comes in many shapes, sizes and areas, and limiting yourself to the area in which you live or the type of property you occupy is the same as putting all of your eggs into one basket. This chapter will explore different types of property and outline the positives and negatives for each.

RESIDENTIAL PROPERTY

We all recognise residential property—the house down the road for sale or the apartment in the city we saw advertised on TV last night. Residential property is any property in which a tenant (or owner) resides and which is zoned residential by the council. For the purposes of investing, a rural property in which a tenant will live, which you buy to make income on those rents alone, would also qualify as residential real estate. The actual zoning may change the way in which you buy and sell this property, but will not change the way it is treated as an investment.

Residential property can have different types of *titles*. A title defines the extent of the property you own, and the certificate of title will record anything that affects the quality of the title, such as mortgages, easements, rights of way and covenants. There are many types of titles (which usually will not affect the tax status of the property) but the three most common for residential property are:

↪ *Old system title*—Also known as common law title, this is usually a house or vacant land where everything within the four boundaries belongs to and is the responsibility of the owner (which in the case of an investment property will be you, the landlord). An old system title will trace the chain of ownership and must be examined each time a property is sold to ensure that there are no other parties with claims to the property.

↪ *Strata title*—Usually applies to a townhouse, flat, villa or apartment, where there is common property which has resulted from the division of the original property into smaller lots and includes the 'air space' belonging to the property. A body corporate with owners as members must be formed to care for this common property, and they will raise levies on the owners to ensure that the common property is maintained.

↪ *Torrens titles*—These have replaced the old system titles and are less complicated, usually only containing a single guaranteed certificate of title. They are most commonly used for division of property where no common ground has resulted, so there would be no need for a body corporate.

There are many other types of titles, with some specific to individual states. Community title is becoming more popular, particularly in Queensland where the Community Titles Act encompasses all strata titled arrangements.

The Investment Benefits of Residential Property

The tax office allows us to *set off* the costs of purchasing a residential investment property against other earned income. Depending on the item, we can either claim a deduction of expenses against the income produced by the property, or we can claim the item against capital gain made at the point of sale.

> The government allows us to set *off* the costs of purchasing a residential investment property...

Most residential properties, and particularly those which were built prior to 1985 carrying no depreciation benefits, will have a negative cash flow where the purchaser is borrowing the entire purchase price plus costs. This is not to say that it is not possible to buy residential property with a positive cash flow—you just have to look a little harder and perhaps go a little further afield than your own back yard!

Positive Features of Residential Property

- Consistent returns, if chosen wisely.

- Always has some value.

- Is accepted as security for borrowing.

- Generally rises in value over time, creating the ability to 'leverage' (see Chapter 5).

- Can insure against some contingent losses using 'landlord's insurance' (see Chapter 8).

Negative Features of Residential Property

- Cannot be quickly turned into cash in the event of an emergency.

- Vacancy can create a strain on cash flow (although positive cash flow will help you manage this risk, as you will see in coming chapters).

- Tenants can cause damage or even flee without paying the rent.

- You may buy in an area which either loses value (very rare) or does not gain value as quickly as other areas. Again, positive cash flow property manages this risk very nicely.

Risk Rating of Residential Property

The risk of residential property as compared to other classes of investment would be low to medium, closer to the low side if you choose positive cash flow. When compared to other property it would be low.

Vacant Land

Vacant land offers an investment opportunity of a slightly different kind. If you purchase vacant land, then you cannot claim any tax deductions unless it becomes income-producing within 12 months of purchase. To achieve this, you would need to erect a dwelling within that time. If you buy vacant land intending to develop it as an investment but subsequently sell it instead, you may be able to claim any capital loss against future capital gains. You will, of course, have a capital gains tax liability if you sold at a profit a block of land which you had purchased as an investment.

When buying vacant land as an investment, your aim would be to either build a dwelling and sell for a profit, or build a dwelling to rent out. You must consider the costs of servicing the interest of any debt during the period of construction to ascertain if this is a viable (or even easy) choice of investment. I would suggest for busy people, stick with an established property from which someone else has already suffered the headaches!

COMMERCIAL PROPERTY

A commercial property is any property which has been zoned by the council as commercial, industrial or retail, and which is leased for the purposes of running a business of some type. This could include shops, offices, warehouses and factories.

When you buy a commercial property, the bank will provide a different type of loan to you and the lending criteria will be different from that of residential lending. Of course, each bank will have a different lending policy so you should call your bank to see what they offer if you are seeking a loan for an investment of this type.

Positive Features of Commercial Property

- Higher rate of return for the money spent.

- A good commercial property can be easier to sell than a residential property.

Negative Features of Commercial Property

- Your commercial property is likely to attract small business owners, as larger businesses very often own their own property. As more than 80% of small businesses go broke in the first five years, you have a high chance of getting tenants who will not see out their lease!

- Often, in order to attract a tenant the landlord must offer a range of incentives, which may include fit-out, rent free periods, etc.

- Commercial property has a markedly higher rate of vacancy for much longer periods of time.

- Commercial property is affected by both the tenancy market and the general state of the economy, as the tenant's business will suffer hardship when the economy is performing poorly.

Risk Rating of Commercial Property

The risk of investing in commercial property would be considered medium when compared to other investment vehicles, and medium to high when compared to other property types.

TOURISM PROPERTY

A tourism property is quite simply the property which you buy for the purposes of letting out to holiday-makers. It presents a difference in that GST must be raised on the tariffs, and remitted to the government by either the property manager or yourself, if you are registered for GST. You can purchase a tourism property in many forms.

1. Holiday Houses

A holiday house (or flat) is any residential property which you choose to let out for short-term accommodation. An advantage of short-term accommodation is that, providing it has been built since depreciation became an allowable deduction (see Chapter 10), you actually get a 4% per year deduction on the construction costs. This can add substantially to your positive cash flow.

I have a house at the beach. It is very old and has been converted to two flats. It rents out for exorbitant rates, but only during Christmas and Easter Holidays. A purchase such as this can work, providing you are sure that the minimum rent you can expect to receive during the short time it is rented is enough to produce a positive cash flow for you, and you can manage this cash flow over the entire year.

2. Holiday Apartments

Most of us are painfully aware of the reputation of holiday apartments, having become familiar with them after reading the many negative stories of hapless investors caught buying a holiday apartment in a trendy tourist area which subsequently could not be tenanted, or which attracted a return far less than expected.

A holiday apartment will usually be in a block of apartments (or villas) with an on-site manager who lets the apartments to holiday-makers. The on-site management may come in several forms—it may be a caretaker arrangement, where the manager is paid from the body corporate levies, or there may be 'management rights'. Management rights are usually offered for sale when the apartments are first put on the market, and involve an arrangement where a person or couple purchase an apartment plus the right to manage the remaining apartments. Unlike a hotel, these apartments are fully self-contained and do not come with a daily cleaning option, leaving the responsibility to the on-site manager or the owner to organise (and pay for) cleaning at the end of each occupancy period (or sometimes on a weekly basis). Rent collected on an apartment like this is given directly to each owner, after costs are deducted.

Holiday apartments are most often strata titled, and the only difference from an ordinary strata titled apartment in the way they are cared for is that the on-site manager lets the apartment out for you (rather than you having to employ a property manager), and of course keeps a closer eye on day-to-day maintenance.

Buying a holiday apartment is fine if you have a realistic opinion of how much money you can make. If 30% occupancy is enough to deliver an even cash flow with anything over that extra, then buying an apartment in an area with low occupancy may still present a viable option. If, on the other hand, you need at least 80% occupancy just to break even, then a purchase such as this needs careful consideration. Even wonderful tourist destinations suffer high vacancy rates in the face of tragic events such as the World Trade Center attacks and the collapse of Ansett.

> An experienced manager should do a good job for you.

Positive Features of Holiday Houses and Apartments

- ➥ A well chosen apartment will let frequently and often provide a very large positive cash flow, particularly when new or nearly new as they often have an abundance of on-paper deductions.

- ➥ An apartment showing a strong history of good returns will be relatively liquid, and increasing returns will impact positively on capital growth.

- ➥ An experienced manager should do a good job for you.

- ➥ Some holiday destinations remain popular for many years, and if you have purchased your property early enough (before the prices become too high) you will enjoy many years of positive cash flow, and a strong growth in value.

- ➥ Sometimes these types of apartments come with a 'free holiday' option for owners, although you do need to understand that this option may come at a price after all, such as no tax deductions or income available during this 'personal use' period.

Negative Features of Holiday Houses and Apartments

↪ Management rights can be purchased by anyone—there are no guarantees you will get someone with experience. (A few years ago I stayed on the Gold Coast in a holiday apartment. My children nicknamed the on-site manager 'the wicked witch of the north', and I admit she did deserve this label! I doubt that we will ever return and we do tell the story to many of our friends. This could have been your apartment!)

↪ Often you are relying on the manager to let out the apartments on a fair, rotational basis. You cannot guarantee that this will occur.

↪ Those apartments with the great views may be the ones most requested. This is fine if you own one of these, but what if yours is at the back overlooking the garbage bins? Many managers recognise this potential problem, however, and are sure to put as many tenants with no special requests into these 'nil view' apartments as they can to balance the letting.

↪ An on-site manager will incur expenses on your behalf, which ultimately come from your rent return. What if they manage the budget poorly, with expenses blowing way out of proportion? This will come from your pocket, and it may be at the cost of your positive cash flow.

↪ You cannot be watching the manager every minute of the day, so you actually have very little control over this arrangement.

Some of these negative features can be managed at the outset with diligent research, as you will see from reading Chapter 6.

Risk Rating of Holiday Houses and Apartments

The risk of investing in a holiday house would be medium when compared to other investment vehicles, and medium when compared to other property types.

3. Hotels, Resorts, Serviced Apartments and Managed Apartments

I have made this separate category to describe those tourism properties where the income is 'pooled' before it is distributed to owners. Where income pooling does not take place, the property would most likely fit into category 2 on page 37.

In July 1998 The Australian Securities & Investments Commission (ASIC) introduced changes to the Corporations Law. Among these changes was a requirement that any 'serviced strata scheme' which required the pooling of an owner's interest in a property to make income, with a resulting pooling of income and expenses, would now be covered by this legislation. In simple terms, this meant that where the intent of the developer was to sell apartments where income and expenses were pooled before distribution, there had to be:

1. A prospectus, outlining the risks and opportunities of the investment.

2. A responsible entity (R/E)—like a fund manager, this person or organisation is retained by the owners (and paid from the pooled income) to oversee the operation of the scheme, and to be sure that any on-site managers hired to run the operation act in the best interests of the owners.
    He or she becomes the employer of the manager on behalf of the owners (shown in the diagram below).

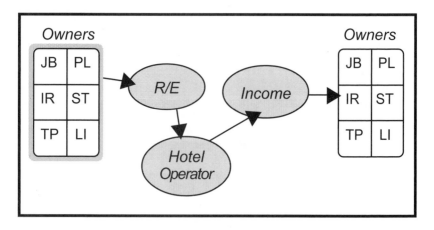

3. Qualified people to sell the apartments—in other words, just like any managed fund or equities security, only people who hold Australian Financial Services Licences (formerly licensed securities dealers) or those people they issue with proper authorities may sell these apartments to potential investors.

In the case where a decision is made to pool the income *after* the sale of the properties, the requirement for a responsible entity still exists.

Generally speaking, with this type of arrangement, the developer will have in place the prospectus and the responsible entity, and will have met all of the ASIC's requirements before even taking the property to market.

Positive Features of Hotels, Resorts, Serviced & Managed Apartments

➥ As with units in a managed fund, income and expenses are pooled and then cut up into shares which relate to the size of your investment. So, if every apartment in the complex is the same size, and there are 50 apartments, then you get 1/50th of the income. In the case where they are different sizes, a formula is worked out for the fair distribution of the income according to the size of your holdings.

➥ Even if your individual apartment remains empty every day of the year, you still get your share—your distribution is not based on the occupancy of your apartment alone.

➥ Often there is a bar, conference room, etc. These will make up part of the common property, of which you own a piece. This means that the pool will also receive the income made from these areas, which ultimately boosts the income you receive. You will, of course, also obtain all of the on-paper deductions (pro rata for your proportion), attached to these areas.

➥ Tax deductions can come from common property as well, often providing a big boost to your on paper costs when you consider depreciation on hotel common area furniture and fixtures.

- Managers are usually paid an income which is a percentage of the profits, rather than a set fee. This is incentive for a manager to perform as profitably as possible.

- Managers in this structure rarely have any equity holdings, and providing their management agreement has an escape clause, a poorly performing manager can be quite easily replaced.

- Because of the high amounts of depreciation available on tourism property (including 4.0% depreciation instead of the 2.5% available on residential property) the amount of positive cash flow can be very high, often providing a hedge against vacancy or lower than expected returns (see Chapter 5).

Negative Features of Hotels, Resorts, Serviced & Managed Apartments

- Many of these have failed over the years due to inexperience and poor performance of the manager.

- The costs of running an entire hotel operation, as opposed to simply letting out apartments, may blow the budget, although this can be grounds for dismissal of the manager by the responsible entity.

- If you have a 'good apartment' you will be affected by the poor performance of a 'bad apartment' because of the income pooling.

- If the hotel is 'seasonal' you may have down time with little income. (This will apply to any tourism investment.)

- Forecast net returns have been found in the past to be unachievable on some properties.

A property investment covered by the Managed Investments Act is not a guarantee of success. The law simply ensures that full disclosure is made prior to you entering a purchase contract—it does not enhance the performance of a property which was never going to make any money in the first place!

Risk Rating of Hotels, Resorts, Serviced & Managed Apartments

The risk of investing in a managed apartment would be medium when compared to other investment vehicles, and medium to high when compared to other property types. The reason for the high rating is that if you choose an area which subsequently does not enjoy success as a tourist destination, you will have low occupancy without a corresponding lowering of costs (as hotels and resorts have a lot of fixed costs). It is important to note that buying one of these types of properties in an area with a proven high occupancy rate will considerably lower the risk.

PROPERTY SYNDICATES AND TRUSTS

I have a bit of a fear of the sea. I love swimming, but I worry that one day I may get eaten by a shark! Strangely though, if there is a large crowd in the water, I will happily swim, safe in the knowledge that if there is a man-eater lurking about, I have lessened the chances of me being the one he picks by increasing the number of choices for him!

Many people feel this way when investing, and prefer the safety which can be offered by managed funds, where you invest your small sum with others who have the same objective as you.

> The risk of investing in a managed apartment would be medium when compared to other investment vehicles...

If you do not want to invest alone yet really like the thought of property, or if you have a lump sum of cash but not enough to get into a property alone, then you may well be interested in one of these two other options.

Property Syndicates

A property syndicate is where a group of people pool their money to buy a property. This can range from a simple structure involving a group of friends (each of whose name would then appear on the title) to a more complex arrangement where an investment manager offers the public the chance to buy shares in a managed syndicate. Under these circumstances, the investment manager making the offer may facilitate the buying of a variety of property, or perhaps a whole complex of apartments or retail stores. They will usually seek what is known as 'non-recourse' finance; that is finance whereby if disaster struck and the property needed to be liquidated, the bank's recourse is limited to the proceeds of the disposal only and does not extend to the assets of the syndicate shareholders.

Even though the individual names of the shareholders are not on the title, an investment such as this is still considered a direct investment from the investors' point of view, and the tax benefits all flow directly through to the investors.

The clear advantage with a managed syndicate is that you have experts choosing and subsequently managing the property, and choosing the best time to liquidate (as syndicates usually have a finite term). In addition, you are able to buy into these syndicates for a small outlay—often as little as $5,000—and the size of the investment when pooled gives access to better performing properties.

> The clear advantage with a managed syndicate is that you have experts choosing and subsequently managing the property...

A property syndicate falls within the Managed Investments Act too, making it subject to the disclosure and responsible entity requirements outlined in the previous section. The disadvantages, however, include a general inability to liquidate outside the predetermined term, and the inability to use your share as security for initial and further borrowings.

Some people use equity in their homes (by getting a larger home loan) to buy shares in a syndicate. If this is what you are planning, be very sure that the net returns (after paying loan interest) make it truly a viable investment and remember that using up your equity in this way will decrease your ability to buy other direct property.

Property Trusts

A property trust is a similar concept, except that the property is bought for the trust and you then buy units in that trust. A property trust is considered an indirect investment because you are in fact investing in the trust, not the property. The taxation treatment will therefore be different.

If you invest in a listed property trust, you have the added benefit of being able to liquidate at any time, as your units can be traded on the stock exchange just like a share. A disadvantage would, of course, be that your unit would also be subject to general sharemarket cycles as well as the overall state of the property market.

Both trusts and syndicates are valuable in the event that you want an exposure to property but do not have the cash or home equity to do so. Trusts are more liquid than syndicates but this liquidity generally comes at the cost of returns, which tend to be lower in trusts. If you have a real interest in investing in these types of vehicles, *How to Invest in Managed Funds* can provide you with much more information about how to do so.

Risk Rating of Syndicates and Trusts

The risk of investing in a property trust or syndicate would be considered medium when compared to other investment vehicles and low to medium when compared to other property.

Conclusion

I have a client called Valerie, who lives in a three-bedroom townhouse in a local suburb, let's call it Centretown. She called me about three years ago and said, "Margaret, I have found a great property to invest in." "Tell me about it," I said. "Well, it's a three-bedroom townhouse in Centretown!" Despite my reservations about its cash flow, she went ahead. Eighteen months later she called again to tell me about a great property she had found, a three-bedroom townhouse in Centretown! I mentioned to her that she had invested fairly heavily in Centretown already (with negative cash flow properties, I might add), and perhaps now was the time to diversify. She went ahead on the emotion of it all, perhaps to justify her own decision for choosing Centretown in which to live. Later she called again, and, you guessed it: "I want to buy this great three-bedroom townhouse in Centretown!" (Centretown has a lot of townhouses.)

Valerie has made two major mistakes—firstly she is too heavily exposed to the one suburb. Even the same area would be too much—it is time she got out and tested the water elsewhere, perhaps in another state. Secondly, Valerie now has four three-bedroom townhouses! If three-bedroom townhouses in Centretown ever go out of favour, she is in big trouble.

It is highly possible to have a large exposure to property while diversifying *within* your property portfolio. All of the property types outlined in this chapter offer viable opportunities to investors who are prepared to do the research. An astute investor will select a range of property types and even venture into a variety of different states! While finding suitable property may seem a huge task, the next chapter can provide you with all of the information you will need to make this job a little easier for you.

> It is highly possible to have a large exposure to property while diversifying *within* your property portfolio.

4   How Do I Find Positive Cash Flow Property?

➠ **Do not let location affect your decisions.**

➠ **Capital gain must take a back seat to the cash flow.**

➠ **Your very first job will be to establish the cash flow.**

➠ **Recognising viable opportunities is only step one in a long process.**

I HAD SOME CLIENTS WHO had seen a property locally which they believed would make a great investment. At the time, I went to great lengths to explain to them the drawbacks of buying the property they were looking at, which had a substantial negative cash flow. I felt the most important factor was that this property would take $72 a week out of their pockets after tax. Since they were on a fairly tight budget, this may well have come from the extra repayments they were making on their personal mortgage, and so slow down the speed with which they gained important equity in their own home. In addition to that they already owned one negatively geared property, bought many years before.

They understood and agreed, and together we sought out quite a few sound, positive cash flow properties. None of them were close by, a few were in the same state but there were an equal number in other states. They said they would think about it and away they went. After following them up several times, I left them to contact me when they were ready to go ahead.

I heard nothing until I discovered that they had actually gone ahead with the local property! In fact, the property in question was in the next street from where they lived. I asked them why they bought this property and the answer was, "It's a good area!"

I am often at a loss as to the real motivation behind decisions like this when, in the face of overwhelming evidence, people go ahead with purchases which may well be wrong for them. Excited as I am seeing people taking responsibility for their own future, I am constantly frustrated when those same people only do half the job!

I believe the reason is that, when it comes to property, we have an automatic tendency to personalise the transaction. Despite the fact that an investment property is an *investment*, purchasers get extremely caught up in the emotions of the exercise. When we buy an investment property in the area in which we live, we are subconsciously justifying our own decision to live there—we live there so it *must* be a good area! We are also forgetting the single most important point about buying property for our future income — that is, the capital gain must take a back seat to the cash flow. Once this is understood, then you will see that a good area, while important, cannot provide income to you if the cash flow is negative.

> ...try to forget about *where* you are buying, and focus on *what* you are buying.

So what is the alternative? Simply try to forget about *where* you are buying, and focus on *what* you are buying. And, if this means buying in another state altogether, then so be it.

I was speaking at the Perth Money Show when a lovely lady came up to me and said, "How can you possibly buy a property you have never seen?" I asked her if she had any shares. "Yes," she said, "Actually I have $50,000 of BHP shares." "Did you visit the company before you purchased them?" I enquired. "Of course not!" she said. I rest my case!

The Point

Buying positive cash flow property is all about being smart in what you do. Yet, finding positive cash flow is not easy. How do you recognise positive cash flow when almost everything you see has a negative cash flow? This chapter will help you to distinguish between the two, and gives some formulas for calculating the cash flow.

Let's Recap

Before we move on, let's be sure that you are very clear on exactly what positive cash flow property is, as only then will you be able to recognise it for yourself.

When you own property as an investment, you will make income from the rent return. You will also have expenses to pay out. Among common expenses will be:

- Rates, council and water

- Possible land tax

- Property management fees

- Body corporate fees

- Repairs and maintenance

- Bank interest and fees

- Insurance.

In many cases, these expenses will exceed the income you can make on the property from the rent, creating a loss, and if you have a period of vacancy, this loss will be exacerbated.

Any loss you do incur can be claimed against other income. So, for a quick calculation, if you apply your top marginal rate of tax to the loss, you can work out how much tax you will get back (or not pay at all, in the case where you have applied for a tax variation —see Chapter 10). If, for example, you make a $3,000 loss, and you pay tax at the 30% rate, then the government will allow you to pay $900 less tax, reducing your loss to only $2,100.

If the property you have purchased was built before 1985, then this is as far as you can reduce your loss. If, however, the property was built after 1985, a range of on-paper deductions may further reduce this loss for you.

What is an On-Paper Deduction?

An on-paper deduction is an item which you can claim against your tax without you having to pay out any money in the first place. Money back, without any money paid out! Let us look at the following two examples.

> Susan pays out $1,000 to repair her property. She pays tax at 30%, so she is now allowed to pay $300 less tax. Her net position is that she has paid out $1,000, but got back $300, so in effect she has only paid out $700.

> Joshua, on the other hand, has a new property which cost $150,000 to build. For 40 years, he is allowed to claim a deduction of tax to the value of $3,750.

Note that this deduction is on-paper only, as it is considered to be the amount at which his property depreciates every year. So, assuming Joshua is also in the 30% tax bracket, every year he gets back $1,125 of his tax, without paying anything out.

These kinds of on-paper deductions can very often not only wipe out the loss, they can actually provide extra money which you did not have before you bought the property. This is then called 'positive cash flow'.

How Does This Work?

Imagine that Susan had total costs on her property which exceeded her income by $3,000 a year. When she bought the property, it was one year old and fully furnished. The owner did not have any receipts for the furniture, or any proof of the costs of construction. This did not matter. Susan employed the services of a quantity surveyor, who for a cost of $400 provided Susan with what is known as a 'depreciation schedule'. This is an itemised list of what the construction costs would have been, and a new 'effective life' for all of the furniture, fixtures and fittings (see Chapter 10 for more information on this). In total, she now has $3,500 which she can claim every year for another 39 years on the construction, and the other depreciable items have a first year deductible amount of $11,000. In total, Susan has $14,500 to add to her 'loss', giving her a total loss of $17,500.

But wait! So far, she has only paid out $3,000 from her own pocket. The $17,500 'loss' will let Susan claim back $5,250 of the tax she has paid on other income. She now has $2,250 (or $43 a week) in her hand! And what will she do with this? This is up to her, but my advice would be to pay it off her mortgage. In later chapters, you will see illustrations of just how big an impact this kind of cash flow can really have on your net position over time.

You Just Can't Find Properties Like That!

I will admit that it is not easy. When I first started buying positive cash flow property I thought I would find thousands in minutes! I can find them when I look, but there is much to know about the calculations as cash flow cannot be determined just by knowing rents and costs. Also, if you are not prepared to look outside of the area in which you live, it is highly unlikely you will find anything.

> If you are not prepared to look outside where you live... it is highly unlikely that you will achieve positive cash flow.

So, why *do* people insist on having a property nearby? I believe there are several reasons:

1. So that they can look at it before buying.

2. So that they can keep an eye on it.

3. Because they feel it is a *good* area.

4. So they do not have to take any leaps outside their comfort zone.

Let's examine these reasons one by one so that they can be excluded once and for all.

1. Looking Before You Buy

When you bought the house you live in now, you probably visited it four or five times before making the final decision. Once you had satisfied yourself that the house suited you from a size and location point of view, and wasn't about to fall down, you were probably going back so that you could measure up for your furniture, and start to visualise yourself living there.

When you buy a house as an investment, you are *not* going to live there. So, what is left to see? If you want to know how many bedrooms, etc. the agent can tell you this, and you can see photos too if you like. If you are concerned about the state of repair, a building inspection will tell you about the structure, a pest inspection will tell you about the termites, and the valuer will tell you about the presentation. So what is left? Nothing, and a visit to inspect will only introduce those emotions which will suddenly make you less clever about the transaction.

> When you buy a house as an investment, you are *not* going to live there.

Hugh is a client of mine whom I have assisted for many years. He gets very emotional about all of his purchases. His last property was bought at auction. He fell in love with it at first sight. The agent expected the property to sell for $300,000, and at that price it was just nudging a positive cash flow. When Hugh started bidding, it was clear that he wanted the property. Did he get it? Yes, but he paid $385,000 for it!

What a disaster! His wife now swears she is going to shackle him to the lounge suite when they decide to make the next purchase. This could have been avoided for Hugh had he realised that this was simply a business transaction, and there are hundreds more opportunities out there offering a very similar return.

2.   *Keeping an Eye on It*

This is a little like looking at the property before you buy it. Personally, I cannot think of anything worse than watching to be sure my tenants are behaving correctly. The last thing I want to worry about is how they are keeping the gardens, or if they are having wild parties. I am fully insured against tenant damage, so why should I worry about my property?

I have a friend who watches her shares every day. She is not a share trader, so she is not doing it for any immediate financial reason. I think she just likes to know whether to have a good night's sleep or not! I have suggested that if she looked at them once every few months and compared the performance to the previous period (she does have blue chip stocks), then she probably will see a favourable result and if not, then she would only have a few days of the year to worry!

I give the same advice to people with property as an investment. Who really wants to be keeping that close an eye on the property? This is what we have property managers for! If there is something to worry about, you can rest assured you will be told about it when the time comes.

3. Because it is a Good Area

What makes the area in which you live a good area? Usually, it is that you like the neighbours, the kids have a school nearby, it is quiet, the streets are cared for or any one of a hundred other reasons.

What makes an area good for investing? Large industry close by, good population growth, strong rental market and much more.

Notice that, while there may be some similarities, there are also some very important differences, which could mean that a good area for you may well not be such a good area for you to find a tenant. Chapter 6 will cover in detail the kinds of questions you should be asking when you buy property as an investment.

4. So You do not Have to Take a Leap Outside of Your Comfort Zone

This is where we really come to the crux of the problem. Let me put this to you with another example.

> Ellen was too frightened to invest in anything. She worked hard and paid off her home by retirement, but did not have much left over. She did receive a $100,000 superannuation

pay-out from the 35 years she worked in her job. She had been promoted quite often, and in her final working year was earning $48,000 per annum.

Upon retirement, she received an aged pension of around $10,000 a year, $3,500 a year in interest on her lump sum from the superannuation, and lived in a house worth over $500,000 (a cottage in the Sydney suburbs).

Eve also worked for the same department as Ellen, and enjoyed a similar career path. In fact, she lived next door to Ellen. However, she bought property every time she could. Ellen thought she took quite a lot of risks, however they were calculated risks. She bought positive cash flow property each time, so she had no cash input of her own. Tragedy struck in her final year of working. A tidal wave struck every area in which she owned investment property and wiped out all of her property holdings except her own home. Insurance companies would not pay out on tidal waves!

Upon retirement, she received a government pension of around $10,000 a year, $3,500 a year in interest on her lump sum from the superannuation, and lived in a house worth over $500,000!

Of course, the reality would be that Eve kept her properties and enjoyed the income stream they provided her. But the moral of this story is this:

If you do nothing, you have a 100% guarantee that you will get nothing.

But, if you do something, then one of two things will happen. You will either get nothing, which you were going to get anyway. Or, you will achieve what you have striven for and enjoy comfort and relaxation all the rest of your days.

How Do You Recognise Positive Cash Flow Property?

Recognising positive cash flow property requires you to do a fair amount of research, and perform calculations to assess the cash flow. The easiest way to perform these calculations is to email us and ask for the free software, available as a download from the internet. This will provide you with some simple calculators, which will tell you very quickly the amount of cash flow (positive or negative) that a particular property can provide. You do, however, need to be in possession of certain figures. If the cash flow is negative, then you will need to go out and start looking again.

Alternatively, you can use a basic formula once you are in possession of the information. But first, let's consider just what you are looking for.

> Recognising positive cash flow property requires you to do a fair amount of research...

The Property Itself

The only criteria is that the property is built after 1985. From this time, you are allowed to claim a 'capital works deduction'. In simple terms, this means the depreciating cost of the building itself. If you are lucky enough to find a property with a construction date between 18 July 1985 and 15 September 1987, then the capital works deduction available is 4% per annum, for a period of 25 years. Anything built from that date on has an allowable deduction of 2.5% for 40 years. Either way the total allowed is, of course, 100%!

The person offering the property for sale (the agent or the owner) should know when it was built, or at least should be able to find this out for you. If they are not sure, phone the local council and ask yourself.

What's Inside?

'Plant' used to produce rental income carries with it an allowable deduction against income earned, at differing rates according to the item. Some items in a rental property are regarded by the tax department as being part of the setting for the rent-producing activity, therefore do not qualify as separate depreciable items in their own right. However, many of these 'non-plant' items may qualify as a capital works deduction. For example, stoves, carpets curtains, washing machines and hot water services are individual items of plant, each with a tax department recommended 'effective life' over which to claim depreciation. On the other hand, built-in kitchen cupboards, clothes hoists, floor tiles, reticulation, tubs and toilet bowls are all considered part of the capital works. A more extensive list of these items can be found in Chapter 10.

Many new or 'off-the-plan' purchases are offered with a full depreciation schedule which covers all items allowable. This does not mean you have to buy a new property, however. You can, as previously mentioned, retain the services of a quantity surveyor for any properties which were built within the allowable period yet do not have a depreciation schedule. Not only will the surveyor make estimations of the value of all claimable items, but fixtures, fittings and furniture get a new effective life from the day you buy the property!

The Rent

As previously mentioned, most properties deliver a return of around 0.10% of the purchase price as a weekly rent amount. While this in itself will not deliver a positive cash flow, a property providing depreciation may well have enough claimable items to wipe out any loss and push you into a positive cash flow.

Any property delivering more than 0.175% of the purchase price as a weekly rent may well deliver a positive cash flow to you without the need for depreciation (known as positive gearing). However, this will mean you have a net gain rather than a loss, and tax will be payable on this gain. In these cases any depreciation available may decrease your gain on paper only and so eliminate any tax responsibilities. Let's look at an example of a property which could deliver a positive cash flow in a number of ways.

> An apartment in Cairns has a value of $120,000 and a rent return of $210 (0.175%) a week. There were also

$5,000 in purchasing costs. The yearly costs for this property are:

Loan interest at 6.25% on $125,000	$7,813
Rates, etc.	$1,000
Body corporate	$200
Property management	$750
Insurance	$300
Total yearly costs	**$10,063**

Assuming this property was built before 1985, the position for the investor would be as follows:

Example One

Gross rent	$10,920
Costs of having the property	$10,063
Net to investor (gain)	$857
Less tax @ 30%	$257
Net cash flow after tax (p.a.)	**$600**

Let's take the same property and assume it was built in 1990, at a cost of $90,000. This will add capital works deductions.

Example Two

Total income	$10,920
Total costs paid by investor	$10,063
Capital works deductions ($90,000)	$2,250
Net to investor (on paper only)	-$1393

Tax back	$418
Cash in hand for the investor	**$1,275**

The investor has received his $10,920 rent, *plus* the $418 tax break (totalling $11,338) but has only paid out $10,063. He now has $1,275 for the year, in his hand, *after* tax!

Sounds great, but let's make this a little more interesting! We'll add $6,000 in year one as depreciation on 'plant', which covers the fixtures, fittings and furniture inside this property.

Example Three

Total income	$10,920
Total costs paid by investor	$10,063
Capital works deductions ($90,000)	$2,250
Plant depreciation	$6,000
Net to investor (on paper only)	-$7393
Tax back	$2,218
Cash in hand for the investor	**$3,075**

The investor has received his $10,920 rent, *plus* the $2,218 tax break (totalling $13,138) but has only paid out $10,063. He now has $3,075 for the year, in his hand, *after* tax!

There are so many things that this extra money could do, including gaining equity in the property to allow the investor to invest again, sooner.

As you can see from the above examples, there was only one case where the investor had to pay *extra* tax. In the other two examples, he received tax back, and he did not need all of that tax refund to fund his loss, as it was more than the loss. If you apply the second and third examples to a property where the cash flow is initially negative, in some cases the depreciation claims will be enough to wipe out that negative cash flow and bring the property into positive cash flow.

Assessing the Cash Flow

By now you have probably become very familiar with positive cash flow. You will know that negative gearing should *never* be accepted. You have seen that just by being sure your property was constructed after 1985, you may be able to get a positive cash flow. Many of you with negatively geared property may even be able to go back and find deductions you did not realise you had!

> ...negative gearing should *never* be accepted.

If you have collected the information you need about a potential property, then you must apply the following formula to assess the cash flow:

1. Work out your current take-home pay (after tax).

2. Apply the following formula to your *gross yearly income* (before tax):

    > Gross income *plus* rent *less* expenses paid *less* capital deductions *less* depreciation

    > EQUALS

    > New taxable income.

    Calculate your new take-home pay using the following formula:

    > Gross income *plus* rent *less* tax on taxable income *less* costs you must actually pay for the property

    > EQUALS

    > New take-home pay.

If the new take-home pay is greater than the old take-home pay, then you have found a positive cash flow property! Don't forget, the free software which you can download can do all of these calculations for you accurately and quickly.

But What About Capital Gain?

Now is as good a time as any for me to deal with the capital gain argument.

When you invest, you must ask yourself 'what am I trying to achieve?' Where property is concerned, the answer will be one of two things. Either:

1. I want to make a large sum of money in a short time, or

2. I want to create an income stream which continues long after I choose to leave the paid workforce—that is, an income for life!

If you are buying property because you wish to make a lot of money in a short period of time, then there are a few things you must know before you commence on this investment strategy.

Firstly, there is a lot of information for you in this book, but some of it will not be appropriate for what you are trying to achieve. Your aim should be to try to select property with a likelihood of a huge capital gain in a short period of time, regardless of the cost to you in the short term. The problems you will face are that it is very hard to forecast capital gain, and a negative cash flow will place a burden on you. By the time you consider the cost to you each week, the purchasing and selling costs and the capital gains tax on 50% of your gain, then the capital gain will in fact have to be very large indeed to make any real profit.

Secondly, a buy-to-sell strategy is riskier than a buy-and-hold strategy, because property is recognised as a long-term investment.

> ...a buy-to-sell strategy is riskier than a buy-and-hold strategy...

This means that the chances of making large amounts of money in short periods of time are generally very slim. And lastly, if this is your aim, then you will only be creating an income stream for retirement if you roll over the profits into income-producing assets.

If, on the other hand, you are buying property in order to provide an income on which to retire, then capital gain is not the prime motivator for you. Of course, it will do no-one any good to have an entire portfolio of properties, none of which gain any value (as this will make leveraging into more property a little harder to achieve). But I would think that if you are careful to choose a good spread of property types, in a wide range of different areas, then you would have to be one unlucky investor to be always choosing nil growth properties (and please let me know where you invest so I can stay away from those areas!).

Later chapters will deal with leveraging, and show you how positive cash flow property can help you to gain equity more quickly even where the property you buy has a less than average capital gain.

BE CAREFUL WHO YOU BUY FROM

I am about to risk the great friendship I have with many real estate agents and even a few developers. In the interests of protecting my readers, however, I would like to issue a few words of warning.

Positive cash flow property is largely not understood. Selling many thousands of copies of *How to Make Your Money Last as Long as You Do* was just a drop in the ocean of people in the property investment market. In most cases, anyone who tells you that they do understand the concept probably only understands positive gearing.

When you begin looking for property, there will be a host of people just waiting to help relieve you of your money. And, nice as they may seem, it is their pocket most of them will be thinking about, not yours. Here's what to look out for.

Real Estate Agents

Most can be very nice people, and one or two who I know really do know their stuff from an investment point of view.

Generally speaking, a real estate agent's job is to get you excited about the aesthetic appeal of a property. They will be able to tell you all about the newly renovated bathroom, they will rush in and open the blinds to let in the light and display the home in all its glory. You, of course, will then 'ooh' and 'aah' and pretty soon you are both caught up in an emotional gathering!

My husband Reuben and I once went on a reconnaissance tour of far North Queensland, as I had heard that this was fertile ground for positive cash flow property. We patiently explained to the agent we met that we were looking to provide an introduction between her and our buyers if she could show us some viable, positive cash flow properties. She quickly gathered together a portfolio of property to show us and off we went.

Everything we saw was positive cash flow, some more than others. The agent had not realised this, not understanding the concept at all. She started with what she thought were the best—sparkling apartments luxuriously furnished with sensational views. Our response had been lukewarm at best as we considered the high cost of upkeep on those soft white carpets and designer curtains, and the possible wear and tear to the exposed timber floors. After a few such properties, she suggested she show us a property which "wasn't very nice". Our reaction when we saw it? Our eyes lit up simultaneously! Here was a property with not only a great cash flow, but vinyl floors and brick walls—tenant proof! We are both very good at keeping our emotions in check but it wasn't long before she caught on and began to realise what made a good property in our eyes.

> Real estate agents are trained to sell property on appeal...

Real estate agents are trained to sell property on appeal and will generally be unable to provide you with any of the important figures you need. However, if you ask the right questions, they should be able to get the answers for you, and you can work out the figures for yourself. A real estate agent is usually very keen to please, I will admit that!

Developers

There are two types of developers—good ones and bad ones! The good ones like to make a profit for themselves doing the right thing for the buyer, and the bad ones don't care about what happens to the buyer after the purchase. The trick is recognising the difference, as on the outside they can both look the same.

In actual fact, shrewd and experienced as I may be, even I cannot tell the difference! I, like many people, have been taken in by a welcoming grin at various times.

Always remember that a developer's aim is to sell you a property and move on. While he or she has responsibilities to provide a structural warranty for a period of years, a property not covered by the Managed Investments Act (that is, most properties) will carry no consumer protection after you have settled. Of course, we would hope that the Trade Practices Act would protect us from blatant 'misleading and deceptive' conduct, but this can be hard to prove and a rather laborious piece of legislation through which to pursue someone. The best advice I can give is do not believe anything a developer (or his or her agent) tells you unless you can substantiate it with your own independent research.

Property Clubs, etc.

These have sprung up around Australia at an alarming rate. Many of them are a little disorganised—I spoke to two representatives from the one 'club' in different states and actually got two different philosophies quoted to me.

The problem is that people selling property as an investment are not covered by the same laws as those who give any other type of investment advice. This is a sad thing, I believe, as a property portfolio is just as legitimate as any other investment portfolio. Yet, anyone can become an 'investment property adviser' without the need for any type of licence or qualification at all (at the time of writing). I personally like to provide property investment advice in a financial advising environment (in the same way that I would provide any financial advice), yet in general, most property investment advisers are unqualified, unlicensed people who are in the game because there are some pretty big commissions offered by developers.

I have been offered property in the past with commissions to me approaching the $20,000 mark (of course, I declined!). When I asked where this money was coming from, I was told, "It's added on to the price, of course!" It is no wonder I have clients coming to me who have, in the past, bought property which is now worth substantially less than they paid for it a year ago (not every one declines these big commissions, it seems).

When dealing with any organisation or property club claiming to be 'experts in property' be sure you know exactly how much they are being paid. They should be happy to disclose this to you. If the commission paid comes off a price which has been set by a proven independent valuation (in effect representing a cut in the developer's own profits, and keeping the property price at fair market value), then it is a fair thing that the salesperson makes some commission. After all, you pay a real estate agent to sell your property, don't you? But don't accept a valuation from the valuer suggested by the salesperson—do some research on local values yourself and if you are really keen, consider having your own valuation done.

> ...don't accept a valuation from the valuer suggested by the salesperson...

Conclusion

If you thought this whole thing was going to be easy, then you may well be thinking again. We have only just begun!

Buying an investment property is an important step in your life and you must be sure that you take a very active role in the process. Recognising viable opportunities is only step one in a long process. The best is yet to come!

Hedging and Leveraging with Positive Cash Flow Property

➠ **The advantages of positive cash flow property go beyond the benefits it can provide for you on a weekly basis.**

➠ **If you buy a property with positive cash flow, you can use the cash flow to accelerate the repayments on any borrowings you may have.**

➠ **Obtaining equity in your property portfolio is very important.**

SO FAR, WE HAVE MANAGED to discover that when you negatively gear property, you lose money every week. Depending on what you do with that property over the long term, it is highly unlikely that your net position, even when you sell, will recover this loss for you.

We also know that positive cash flow property *gives* you money, each week. On the surface, the benefit would appear to be that you now have more disposable dollars in your hand. For some of you, this may make life a little easier today, while you are working on your plans for tomorrow.

In fact the advantages of positive cash flow property go far beyond the benefits it can provide for you on a weekly basis. Positive cash flow property can not only help you to get where you are going much faster, it also provides a useful hedge against many of those things people worry about when they invest in property, such as interest rate rises, occupancy levels and rent return decreases.

When you take a lump sum of cash and invest it for your future, you will generally have the basic aim to 'hedge' against inflation. Most investors want to be sure that, when they need their money in the future, it will at least have the same buying power that it has today. Any returns over and above this will be 'growth', and result in the money being able to buy more tomorrow than it could today. The risk for these investors is investing their money and having it grow slower than inflation, or worse still, disappearing altogether!

The majority of people do not have lump sums to invest. We lead full and busy lives, yet for most people living from week to week is all that they can manage. Therefore, investing for these people has a different focus—that is providing an income for retirement, and perhaps accumulating assets which, if needed, can be turned into cash. Property is one of the few ways by which this can be achieved. Property, over time, will always show growth. Property will never 'go broke'. Property can provide a relatively stable income. Most importantly, you do not need a cash lump sum to buy property. And, if you buy positive cash flow property, not only will you add to your current cash flow *every* week, you will have purchased an investment which provides a hedge against many of the common risks of property and a leverage into more property.

> Property will never 'go broke'.

The Point

The aim of this chapter is to allay some of the common fears people have when they buy property by demonstrating the true power of positive cash flow property. It will show how positive cash flow property can reduce many of those risks which are inherent when choosing property as an investment.

The Common Fears

When people approach me about buying property as an investment, they usually have three common fears.

They are:

1. That bank interest rates will rise and they will not be able to afford to keep the property.

2. That they will not be able to get a tenant, or will have periods without a tenant.

3. That they will not be able to achieve the level of rent they need to cover the expenses on the property.

While positive cash flow property cannot take away these risks, it can certainly help you to manage them, effectively lowering the risk for you and allowing you to worry a little less about these things.

Let's consider these fears, and look at how positive cash flow property can impact upon them.

1. Bank Interest Rates Will Rise

This is not only a common fear, but a highly valid one. With five interest rate cuts in 2001 and two rises in 2004, we can never know where we are as far as interest rates go.

Many of you will remember the high interest rates of the eighties. Reaching 18%, investing with borrowed funds was not viable. It was all we could do to manage the mortgage payments on our own homes. While we felt this in our hip pockets, building stalled and we were plunged into an economic recession.

Despite assurances to the contrary by our government, we cannot be entirely sure that we will never see these high rates again. However, even a small rate rise can make many people nervous and cause them to close up shop on their investment plans.

Thank goodness for positive cash flow property! Imagine a property which gave you $50 a week in your pocket ($2,600 a year). If an interest rate rise of 1% added $2,000 a year to your repayments, you would still be ahead, even before any tax deduction, as you have room in your cash flow to meet this increase. Consider the following illustration.

Paul's property gives him $50 a week in positive cash flow. He has a debt of $180,000 against this investment property. Interest rates rise three times in just six months, and by the end of the year his rate is 1.25% higher than it was last year. Paul must pay out $2,250 more than he paid the previous year.

As this situation increases his expenses, he will be allowed to make a higher claim for bank interest deductions this year than he did last year. At the 30% tax rate, this means he will get back an extra $675 in tax. His net position will be:

Current surplus funds (cash flow) per year	$2,600
Less *extra repayments on the loan*	$2,250
Plus *extra tax back*	$675
Net cash to Paul	**$1,025**
	(almost $20 a week)

Of course, this is not ideal as he is now getting less cash in hand. But, the point is he is *still* getting cash in hand. Had he owned a negatively geared property, he would now be losing even more than he lost before! Let's see the same illustration for Jarrod, who has a $65 a week (after tax breaks) negative cash flow.

Current loss per year	$3,380
Plus *extra repayments on the loan*	$2,250
Less *extra tax back*	$675
Net cash from Jarrod's pocket	**$4,955**
	(more than $95 a week)

I usually like to use 30% as the top marginal rate of tax when working out most calculations. This covers all of those people earning between $20,601 and $52,000. Of course, if you earn more than this, your benefits will be greater. If you earn less than this, they will be smaller. All in all, the point remains the same—positive cash flow provides a hedge against rising interest rates in a way that negatively geared property cannot.

When I buy property for myself, I always work out just how high the interest rates can go before I eliminate my cash flow and begin to see a negative. Usually, it is quite high, and this can often help me choose between two properties—the one with the biggest margin is the one I buy (see, no emotions at all!).

2. *Periods of Time Without a Tenant*

If you are worried that you will not get a tenant at all, then you are either worrying quite needlessly, or you have chosen a very risky area. If you are worried about periods of vacancy, then here is where positive cash flow property can once again come to the rescue.

Simply work out how many weeks a year you will need to have the property tenanted in order to keep the cash flow at least $1.00 positive. Some of my properties need 40 weeks, others less. My holiday house needs 8 weeks!

Remember Paul? He has a positive cash flow of $50 a week at present. This is based on 52 weeks tenancy, as he has a permanent tenant on a long lease (at $250 a week). Imagine that the tenant moves out. How many weeks a year can Paul have no tenant? There is no simple formula (although our free software can do this calculation for you, providing you know all of the variables). For Paul, let's imagine that it takes him 12 weeks to find a new tenant.

The difference in his income for 40 weeks of tenancy is $3,000. This means he will have a loss of $3,000 more than he had before. This $3,000 extra loss will result in $900 more tax back for Paul. His net position is as follows:

Current surplus cash (cash flow)	$2,600
Less *new loss*	$3,000
Plus *extra tax back*	$900
Net cash to Paul	**$500**

Even at 40 weeks a year occupancy, Paul still makes a positive cash flow. Positive cash flow property provides a hedge against periods of vacancy.

3. Cannot Achieve the Quoted Level of Rent

One thing most investors worry about is that the expected rent return will not be realised. Where the cash flow is negative, any rent achieved which is less than required will further impact on the loss on the property.

Often investors buy property directly from the developer, and sometimes off the plan. In cases like these it can be very hard to know if the returns quoted truly are achievable or sustainable.

> Kelly is a client who purchased a resort apartment with a quoted return of 8%. The reality is that she has never seen anything higher than 5%! This would be enough to send most investors screaming off into the woods, but not Kelly. The property had such a high cash flow that she has been able to absorb the difference into the positive cash flow.

Let's have a look at what would happen with Paul if he could not get the rent he needs.

> Paul expects $50 a week positive cash flow. This is based on the fact that the salesperson told him that the property would rent for $250 a week. When the time came, the best he could do was $210, which was a far cry from the quoted return. His net position is as follows:

Expected return per annum	$13,000
Cash flow at expected return ($50 a week)	$2,600
Actual return	$10,920
Extra loss made	$2,080
Extra tax back	$624
New cash flow	**$1,144** ($22 a week)

From this example, you can see that Paul still has a long way to go before he eliminates his positive cash flow. Positive cash flow property provides a hedge against falling or lower-than-expected rent returns.

This can also mean that, in times of lower than average occupancy levels, the owner of a positive cash flow property can afford to drop rent to attract the small pool of tenants that are available. This certainly makes this type of property far more competitive than negatively geared property, on which losses will be compounded if the rent is lowered.

Remember that positive cash flow is not an automatic recipe for success, and it certainly does not remove the risk of investing altogether. All investing carries risk and positive cash flow property is no exception. It is nice to know, however, that at least you have some room to move when the chips are down. Have a look at the last pages in this book for information about a program which is available from Destiny which can calculate for you minimum occupancy levels, rent returns and the impact of interest rates on any property you may be considering.

> Positive cash flow property provides a hedge against falling... rent returns.

Leveraging With Positive Cash Flow Property

I had a somewhat lengthy discussion with a gentleman at a seminar I recently conducted. He ardently asserted to me that we *had* to have capital gain on our property, and that it needed to be our prime motivator. That being the case, the only place to invest was in a capital city. This same gentleman believed that positive cash flow property was not possible and no evidence to the contrary was going to convince him otherwise. When I told him that I owned *no* property in the city, yet had a portfolio of perfectly respectable, strongly performing property which did, in fact, deliver to me a positive cash flow every week, his answer was, "Rubbish!"

There is a very old school of thought which believes that property as an investment provides benefit only through its capital growth.

While I agree that capital growth is important, I would like to show you how carefully buying positive cash flow property can in fact still provide you with a good opportunity to leverage. Always remember what we are trying to achieve—an income for life, not lump sum profits in the short term.

How does Leveraging Work?

Leverage in these circumstances refers to the process of using the growing equity that you get in a property portfolio to continue to buy more property. This can best be explained with a personal example.

> When we purchased the house in which we now live seven years ago, we paid $370,000. After one year, it was worth $410,000, which meant that, without expending any personal effort or money, we were worth around 10% more. This extra 10% was enough to form the deposit on another property.

Over the years we have added to our property portfolio in this way and today have a portfolio worth well over $4 million. If this year we have another 10% increase in the values, then, without expending any personal effort or money, we will be worth an extra $400,000. This is enough to form the deposit on three more properties.

> Always remember what we are trying to achieve—an income for life...

This is what leverage is all about. In essence, leveraging this way is providing you with free money. And, since you are already getting free money from the positive cash flow of the property, you are getting a lot of free money!

Didn't You Say Capital Growth Was Not Important?

In fact, I have said that capital growth is not *the* most important feature. The important feature is to get equity in your property as quickly as you can.

When you buy property, you are most likely to get *some* capital growth, and some areas will provide a greater level of growth than others. But, capital growth is not the only way to get equity in your property.

If you buy a property with positive cash flow, you can use the cash flow to accelerate the repayments on any borrowings you may have. Accelerating the repayments means that you are owning your property faster. And, if you are owning it faster, you are gaining equity in it faster.

Take a look at the following illustration which will show you how Teresa and Ted accelerated their personal mortgage repayment simply by buying a positive cash flow property. Note that this is a real client (of course the names have been changed!) and this is what we were able to help them to do.

Teresa and Ted currently have a principal and interest loan of $165,000 against the home in which they live, valued at $250,000. They are paying an interest rate of 6.07%, and they pay $1,050 a month as a repayment, which is $80 a month more than the bank actually requires. Ted earns $50,000 gross per annum and Teresa earns $15,000. They have yearly personal expenses of $34,000, not including income tax or loan expenses.

Pathway 1

If they continue on the current pathway they will:

⇒ Have a total loan term of 21.42 years.

⇒ Pay interest of $129,876.

⇒ In total, repay $294,876 to the bank!

Pathway 2

Let's assume that Teresa and Ted switch over to a 'line of credit loan' (see Chapter 9) and use 'mortgage reduction principles' (see Chapter 12). They will now:

⇒ Have a total loan term of 10.33 years.

➠ Pay interest of $59,951.

➠ Repay a total of $224,951 to the bank.

Pathway 3

We will now take this one step further, and assume that Ted and Teresa buy a positive cash flow property every time their equity allows them to. Remember, they pay nothing out of their own pocket (in fact they get money in their pocket). The property used as an illustration is a real property. The details of the property are:

Investment property price	$119,750
Investment property depreciation yr. 1	$5,300
Rent (p.a.)	$12,000
Investment property yearly expenses	$4,000

Ted and Teresa will now:

➠ Buy an investment property in months: 0, 16, 32, 43, 53, 61, 72, 80, 85 and 95 (ten in all).

➠ Have a personal debt loan term of 7.92 years.

➠ Repay interest on their personal debt of $42,317.

➠ In total repay to the bank $207,317 for their personal debt and have exposure to the rising market with ten properties.

Not only has positive cash flow property managed to enhance a loan term which had already been improved through basic mortgage reduction, it has allowed Teresa and Ted to become widely exposed to a property portfolio which will become their income for life.

The Melting Pot

When you borrow to invest, in effect your property becomes a part of a big melting pot. Rather than think of your debts as they apply to each property, you should be thinking of your debt as one amount, and the total value of your properties as another. This way, extra repayments from surplus funds or from the positive cash flow are applied to the debt wherever it is needed most.

In the case where you have your own personal mortgage still to repay, you would put all excess funds and cash flow into this part of your debt—paying interest only on the investment part. Where all debt is investment debt, surplus funds go there.

As you can see, this will help to provide equity more quickly, and so allow you to invest again a lot sooner.

The problem with capital growth is that we can never be sure of it. If the agent tells you that the area has high capital growth, he or she is simply reporting history to you—and you can never be sure that you have not actually missed the growth.

Of course, you can be lucky. I bought a villa in 1996 for $190,000 at a time when not much was happening in that area (and not a lot was expected). For no real reason this suburb became quite trendy, and in 2001 the property was worth $325,000. Now, I may seem clever to some people but this was sheer luck, and it could have gone the other way. I might add that at $190,000 the property was positive cash flow, but since rent return had only increased by $20 during that time, at $325,000 it most definitely would not have been. Most people bought into this suburb after the unexpected boom in prices because they were hearing about the great growth. Those buying more recently have not benefited from this growth as the area has not moved much at all in over 12 months.

> We cannot be sure of capital growth but we can be sure of cash flow.

We cannot be sure of capital growth but we can be sure of cash flow. I would rather have a property with little chance of big growth yet a positive cash flow than I would one with anticipated growth but a negative cash flow. If the growth does not materialise then I would be left footing the bill each week, unable to liquidate as I would lose too much. A person with ten properties all getting good growth cannot ease negative cash flow if it gets too much without liquidating some of the property. At least with the positive cash flow I will still have money each week which I can then use to obtain the equity that I need to invest further.

If you spread your property types and areas, you would have to be very unlucky to always choose nil growth areas. Overall, your portfolio would have a better-than-even chance to at least meet, and possibly exceed, average growth levels for property, and you will have cash left over each week.

Don't Buy One to Pay the Other

Dan bought a positive cash flow property with which he was very happy. It was in another state but with $86 a week positive cash flow he was not too worried about this. Six months later Dan called to say he wanted to buy the property next door to where he lived. It was going to cost him $72 a week from his own pocket. "You can't afford that," I told him. "Yes I can," he said, "My other property will pay for it for me!" He was right, but this is almost as bad as the illustration I gave in my first book, where a client took a part-time job to fund the loss on her property!

There is not much point in getting a positive cash flow property if you are only going to use the money to fund a loss elsewhere. Of course, if you already have negatively geared property, then this could be a legitimate way to neutralise the situation. But please, don't throw away your new profits by buying a negatively geared property. Commit to positive cash flow and refuse anything less!

Your Net Worth

Over time, positive cash flow property can have quite a remarkable effect on your net worth. I have done many financial analyses for people which show them how much greater their net worth can be by choosing to buy positive cash flow property each time they were able, rather than just pay off their homes and save the extra cash.

No doubt you have seen advertisements for 'free investment seminars' conducted in a venue close to you. You may even have been 'tele-marketed' to attend one such seminar. In almost every case, these seminars are conducted by either developer's agents, property salespeople, or sometimes finance brokers looking to make some extra income by selling property.

The seminar will most likely outline for you the benefits of buying one of the properties on offer. At some time, the seminar presenter may even go so far as to suggest to you that buying a negatively geared investment property can speed up the rate at which you pay off your personal mortgage.

This is not true! If you have *less* money than you had before you bought the property, how can you pay *more* into your mortgage?

Many years ago people were advised to pay all of their funds, including property rents and personal incomes, into their own personal mortgage, and let the interest on their investment loans capitalise. This meant that the interest added to the balance each month, rather than being paid, resulting in an increasing investment debt.

If you look closely at this option, you can see how potentially disastrous this can be—admittedly you pay off your own house in double quick time but what happens to your investment loans? Not only do they go backward, but you begin to pay interest on your interest which, when compounded over the years, can be quite devastating!

Since all debt should be considered in its entirety anyway, you are simply shifting the debt. And, since the only reason you would choose to do this would be to maximise your tax deductions, I can assure you that the tax department takes an extremely dim view of taxpayers who avoid tax in this manner.

Increase Your Net Worth

Positive cash flow can, however, have the opposite effect, and really can help you to increase your net worth at a greater rate. Let's revisit Teresa and Ted. We know that they have rapidly decreased the time in which they will pay out their personal debt. In doing so, they will also obtain quite a substantial portfolio of property. Of course, there will be debt attached to this property. But, let's now take a look at what their net worth truly could be after a 12-year period, given the three pathways outlined earlier. For this exercise, we will consider that expenses and income inflate at 3% per annum, and property inflates at 6% per annum. We will also consider that any savings attracts 2% interest.

Pathway 1

If Teresa and Ted continued with the principal and interest loan, paying $80 more a month than required by the bank, and saved all surplus funds, after 12 years they would:

➡ Have a property worth $503,049.

➡ Have a debt of $98,415 still remaining.

➡ Have savings of $51,539.

➡ Have a total net worth after 12 years of $456,173 ($503,049 – $98,415 + $51,539).

Pathway 2

If Ted and Teresa were to switch to a line of credit, and put all of their funds into this line of credit and save all surplus funds once the debt was finalised, after 12 years they would:

➡ Have a property worth $503,049.

➡ Have no debt remaining (as it was paid out in 10.33 years.)

➡ Save $28,455 in the 1.67 years left after the debt is finalised.

➡ Have a net worth after 12 years of $531,504 ($503,049 + $28,455).

You can see that even with mortgage reduction, pathway 2 is only slightly better than pathway 1. I would also like to point out that, generally speaking, people do not commit their excess funds to saving in this manner, so in both of the above pathways it is highly likely that little or no savings will result.

Pathway 3

If Teresa and Ted were to switch to a line of credit and purchase the positive cash flow properties outlined earlier, after 12 years they would:

➠ Have a total debt of $1,043,030.

➠ Have property totalling $2,334,052 in value.

➠ Have a net worth after 12 years of $1,291,022 ($2,334,052 – $1,043,030).

This is more than double what they could have achieved had they not bought the property. Also note that:

➫ This strategy has cost them nothing from their own pocket.

➫ The properties did not need to have high purchase prices nor did they need to achieve a high level of capital growth (being just 6% per annum).

➫ Nothing about their lifestyle needed to change.

➫ They did not have to be clever, nor know when to 'trade' their investments as they may have needed to do with other investments.

➫ Their maximum exposure was never more than 80% of their total equity, making the entire proposal quite low risk.

➫ If they choose to retire after 12 years, they could sell enough of their portfolio to pay out their debt, if they wished to be debt free. Even at only a 6% rent return, they would still have over $47,000 a year income from the remaining rental properties, own their own home and have no personal debt to support!

This was not an unusual client—in fact Teresa and Ted are quite typical of most of our clients and the strategy which we developed for them was not unlike what we usually achieve for most people.

How Can You Sleep?

I am often asked how I can sleep with all of that debt. I believe that being afraid of debt is the very thing which holds many people back from investing. I never look at what I owe—I prefer to look at what I own. Looking at Teresa and Ted, they may owe $1 million, but they *own* almost $1.3 million! This is a comfortable position to be in, and the debt at this stage is quite inconsequential, representing just 44% of the total equity. Even if they did get in to some kind of financial difficulty, their strong equity position would mean that they could sell up almost everything and still own not only the house they live in but enough properties to produce a good income.

The Power of Your Capital

Obtaining equity in your property portfolio is very important. When people think about their net worth, they usually think in terms of assets minus liabilities.

But, have you ever stopped to think about the true power of that equity, or capital? It is worth more to you than the dollar value it represents.

> Diane and Juliette are friends who each have a home worth $250,000, on which they owe $150,000. They both apply to the bank to extend the loan up to 80% of their homes' valuations, or $200,000.
>
> Diane decides to spend her money—she takes an overseas trip, and buys air conditioning, a new television and a pool.
>
> Juliette uses her $50,000 to buy a property worth $200,000—borrowing a further $160,000. She makes sure that the property is positive cash flow and pays no money from her own pocket.
>
> Five years pass. What are their respective positions?

The value of Diane's $50,000 is whatever it was worth five years earlier *plus* the interest she has paid on it each year. Assuming 6.25% interest, so far it has cost her $65,625 to have the things she bought. None of the physical assets are actually worth a lot today, as they have depreciated considerably.

Let's add to this the lost opportunity from not using this money more wisely by investing it. Imagine that Diane had placed this money into a managed fund earning 8% per annum, compounding, instead of spending it. After five years she would have had over $23,000 in income and growth. In total, spending this money as she has done has, in effect, cost her almost $39,000! She is now $89,000 behind where she was five years ago.

The value of Juliette's $50,000 is much more exciting. Assuming that Juliette's property has gained in value by 5% each year, by the end of the fifth year, it has a value of $255,000. Note that she has used $50,000 to gain access to a capital growth on $200,000.

Even if Diane had invested her $50,000 in managed funds, then she would only be seeing a return on that $50,000. Juliette's $50,000 is exposing her to a return of 5% of $200,000, every year! After five years her money has returned her 110%.

This is the true investment power of your dollar when used to buy positive cash flow property, and the reason why borrowing to invest can be such an important aspect of your investment strategy.

Conclusion

Property can provide you with a range of benefits which other investment vehicles simply cannot. Being careful in your choice will minimise those traditional risks which investors use as excuses not to buy property.

Property provides a regular income, substantial tax breaks and access to capital gain, and borrowing can allow you to increase the power of your capital. It also provides you with the comfort of having an investment which you can see and touch, and which you do not have to use any of your own cash to acquire.

> Property can provide you with a range of benefits which other investment vehicles simply cannot.

6 Buying Positive Cash Flow Property – Due Diligence

➟ **Due diligence is just as important with property as it is with any other investment.**

➟ **Know what type of property you want before you start looking.**

➟ **Your property does not need to be close to where you live.**

➟ **Proper research will prevent you from becoming emotionally involved in the process.**

I HAVE SPOKEN TO PEOPLE who have had very bad experiences with property. I will not pretend that property is the be all and end all of investing, and it is not risk free.

A new client of mine phoned to excitedly report that he had found exactly the right property in which to invest. He proudly informed me that he had asked all the right questions and had received answers he was more than happy with. "Well done," I said. "Who did you ask these questions to?" "The salesperson, of course," was his reply!

When people have a bad experience with property it can be bad luck. But more often than not, it is because there was not adequate research done in the beginning. Even where the right questions are asked, they are often asked of the wrong people. Of course the salesperson is going to tell you what you want to hear! They want to sell you a property.

People who buy shares and managed funds usually carry out what is known as

> Even where the right questions are asked, they are often asked of the wrong people.

due diligence. This is finding out as much background information as they can to help them make an informed decision. While due diligence can not make an investment more likely to perform, it can mean that they recognise a bad investment before they go too far with its purchase.

The Point

Due diligence is just as important with property as it is with any other investment. Strangely, people seem to forget their common sense when it comes to buying a property, most probably due to that emotional factor we previously discussed. This chapter will provide you with a host of questions which must be asked before proceeding with any property purchase.

Before You Find a Property

Before you even begin to look, take out a piece of paper and try to determine just what you are looking for. If you have a partner to consider, it is important to both agree on what you want before you go out and get too attached to a property (which, of course, you will not do anyway!).

It may be that you will not consider a particular property type—you may not like tourism property, or residential may not be for you. It could be that you will take anything with a positive cash flow (somewhat like myself!).

Once you know what you want, think about the price range you are willing to consider. For those people who have a small amount of equity, you will be limited by this. Lender's mortgage insurance can provide you with a slightly higher loan-to-valuation ratio, but as I have mentioned before, I do not recommend this. For those who have greater flexibility in price, you need to set a maximum limit.

When doing this, keep your feet on the ground and remember what you are trying to achieve. When I watch those 'auction shows' on television and see people paying in excess of $450,000 for a single 'investment unit', it makes me shudder. This is a lot of money to be spending on one investment, and it is like putting all of your eggs in one basket.

Spreading Your Investment

If $450,000 was your price range, you would be far better to buy three $150,000 properties, all of a different type and all in a different area. This way, you will be able to:

↪ Spread your investment and therefore diversify your property portfolio.

↪ Access differing levels of capital gain.

↪ Have your investments in smaller 'chunks' so that, in the event that you would like to liquidate now or in the future (or perhaps are forced to through an unexpected event), it may be possible to liquidate only some of your portfolio. You can then still stay in the market with the rest.

↪ Get a positive cash flow, as the higher the purchase price the more difficult it can be to get positive cash flow.

I always like to choose my property from the lower third of the market in terms of price for the following reasons:

↪ There are more buyers in this market, so forced liquidation will be easier.

↪ There is more choice in this market.

↪ There are more tenants looking for properties in this market.

↪ In the event that I have to reduce the rent I am seeking by, say, 10%, this would represent a smaller amount.

↪ In the event that I have to drop my price if selling, then I do not have as much to lose.

Once you are sure you know what type of property you may want, you are ready to go and look. Try not to become too attached to a particular area—you will remember that the area (and so its capital growth potential) is not as important as the cash flow.

Following is a list (although not exhaustive) of questions you must ask before you even consider making an offer to buy.

> Once you are sure you know what type of property you may want, you are ready to go and look.

Question 1. What is the Cash Flow?

By now I am beginning to sound like a broken record. By the end of this book I plan to have you so focused on positive cash flow that you dream about it! I mention this question here because I would like to make one thing very clear (again!)—if the cash flow is not positive, then you should move on and look at something else. Go no further, and do not waste any more of your precious time looking at this property because it is not for you.

To determine the cash flow on the property you will need to know:

⇝ The lowest rent return possible.

⇝ The interest rate on the loan you will establish.

⇝ The full costs to purchase, including stamp duty and conveyancing.

⇝ The amount to be paid for council and water rates.

⇝ If there are any body corporate fees.

⇝ If you will need to pay for garden maintenance.

⇝ A ballpark figure for landlord's insurance.

⇝ The original construction costs (this may need to be an estimate if these figures are not freely available).

⇝ The costs (or value) of any fixtures, fittings and furniture.

To those items I would throw in an amount for repairs, depending on the age of the property. Even a new property may still have repairs—in the first two years of owning a new unit in Cairns I had around $900 in incidental repairs.

Once you have these figures, use the software which you have downloaded from us to determine the cash flow for you—and remember that this is a personal thing and depends on your top marginal rate of tax.

If the cash flow is positive, then you are ready to move on to the following questions.

Question 2: What is the Vacancy Rate in the Area?

This is not an easy question for which to get an answer. Real Estate Institutes in some states have great websites which actually provide occupancy levels for areas in that state. Some of these institutes can provide this information if you telephone.

Barring this, you may need to carry out a little discrete research of your own. Try phoning a property manager in the area, and saying you are thinking of using him or her to manage a property you are purchasing. Then ask how many other properties he or she manages, how many are at present empty and what is the average time taken to fill a vacancy. Also check with this person whether the rent return you are looking for is achievable. Keep this person's number, because, as you will see in a later question, you may need it again.

Question 3: What is the Competition?

The answer to this question depends on the type of property you are buying.

If you are buying a house, then the answers you obtained from the property manager should give you some idea if there is a demand for this type of accommodation. If you are buying an apartment or unit, then I would also phone the local council and ask for a list of development application approvals (some councils charge for this). If I was considering purchasing an apartment, and I discovered approval over the next three years for 500 more apartments nearby, then this may cause me to reconsider if other evidence shows me that the population is not increasing very rapidly.

Development application approvals should also give you an indication of any future tourist accommodation which is being planned, in the event that you are seeking to purchase this kind of accommodation.

Question 4: What Other Improvements are Being Planned for the Area?

While you are talking to the council, try to establish if there are any plans for shopping centres, schools, day care centres and parks.

These are all reliable indicators of a growing community, and a community which is growing will have a steady stream of tenants available. Be very careful in the case where there is a lot of building activity in a remote area and full occupancy on rental properties—this may mean that properties are full of short-term tenants who have been brought in to work on the new developments, and once completed these people may be just as quick to depart.

Question 5: What is the Population Growth Like?

I bought my first investment property on the strength of the enthusiasm of the salesperson (this is why I am so clever about what *not* to do!). He told me that 10,000 new people a year move into the area, and he was telling the truth. What he did not tell me was that 12,000 people a year move out! My tenants turn over every six months as a result of this itinerant population. If the population growth is nil, this could signal future difficulties in finding a suitable tenant over the long term.

> If the population growth is nil, this could signal future difficulties...

Question 6: Why do People Live in This Area?

Find out what attracts people to the area in the first place. If it is because of industry, make sure that it is not an industry that has a reputation for closing large plants and retrenching hundreds of workers. Towns relying on one type of industry quickly become ghost towns (or at least a skeleton of what they were) once the industry supporting it shuts its doors.

Question 7: Is the Property Tenant Friendly?

This is where being unemotional is most important. A house with fresh, new beige carpets, shiny new furniture, pretty rose gardens and an in-ground pool makes a great place to live—and a dreadful place to let out. That is not to say that tenants will not care for your property—I am pleased to say I have had some wonderful tenants in my properties. However, the reverse can also occur, and if you ensure that there is nothing to cause too much damage to, then you will have a lot less to worry about.

Vinyl or tiles instead of carpets is good, solid brick or besser block walls as opposed to plaster is tough, laminate cupboards (rather than timber) in the kitchen stand up well. Air conditioning may be nice but is costly to maintain (as regular services are needed), and other 'extras' are just not necessary (although, in the case of air conditioning, it may be a must in a tropical climate). Low maintenance gardens are an absolute necessity.

Question 8: Does it Have Furniture?

Whether to furnish a property or not, or whether to buy a furnished property or not, depends entirely on where the property is located. For example, my unit in Cairns is fully furnished. This is because Cairns has an itinerant population who come mainly for a working holiday. Few people want to pay the high costs of transporting their furniture to Cairns! On the other hand, another of my long-term let properties is not furnished, as the tenants it attracts prefer to bring their own furniture. Of course, a holiday let property will need to be furnished.

Furniture can add a considerable amount of money to your cash flow through depreciation, yet in many cases it can make your property harder to lease.

Question 9: Is There Transport Nearby?

A large number of tenants may not have their own car, and so transport nearby may be important. We have on our property register some units marketed to seniors. It was vital that these properties had transport close by as many aged people prefer not to drive.

On the other hand, transport may not be an issue for you. It will depend largely on the area you are buying in and the type of client you will be trying to attract.

Question 10: What Condition Is It In?

I know of property seminars where the attendees are encouraged to buy old properties and then do them up. It is claimed that

$10,000 spent can add as much as $50,000 to the price, which would be of great benefit to investors seeking to sell for a profit or leverage again quickly. I have seen very few examples of this really being the case, and those that I have seen are usually those properties bought by professional property traders who use all of their time, expertise and contacts to really make some changes to the property.

Generally speaking, money spent on cosmetic renovations will not add any more than what was spent, and often far less. And, in those cases where value is truly added, once again capital gains tax will play havoc with these gains in the event that you sell for the profits.

Most of the people who consult me about property just want something they can forget about—renovating an investment is just too hard. These days people hardly have enough time to maintain their own home, without also having the job of fixing up another property.

When you buy property far from where you live, you cannot just go and look at every property which you *might* like to buy. So, how can you be sure that it is in good condition?

Of course you would start by asking the salesperson. In the case of an established property, a salesperson should be able to give you a pretty good idea of the condition. To check on this opinion, go back to the property manager you called earlier. Ask if he or she could possibly go out and assess its rental potential for you, and do a condition report as well. A manager at all keen to obtain the rights to manage the property will do this quite happily. Any property manager who does this for you would be well in the running to get the management job!

You can go to the cost of having an independent valuer go and look for you. This costs around $200 (providing your bank orders this for you) and you will not need to have another one done at the time you apply for the loan.

A valuer will provide quite a lengthy report, including his or her opinion of the property's condition. This is not a building inspection, however, so a valuation showing that a property has a good presentation does not mean that there are no structural problems.

Once you have decided to buy, it is best to pay to have a building inspection done, as well as a pest inspection (see next chapter). When I buy property which I am not going to inspect myself, I usually take the route of getting the local property manager to inspect *and* I pay for a valuation to be done before I make an offer and begin to negotiate. If the purchase subsequently falls through, I consider this to be one of the costs of investing, which in the big picture is a very small drop in the ocean.

> Once you have decided to buy, it is best to pay to have a building inspection done...

Question 11: Is There a Body Corporate?

If you are buying a property which has a body corporate (that is, a strata titled property), you will have body corporate levies as well as a sinking fund contribution to meet. The levies are raised to carry out the ongoing maintenance of the common ground—such as lawn mowing, gardening and general cleaning. The sinking fund is in place to manage any long term repair work, such as roofing or pipe replacements, pathway repairs, etc. At any time during your ownership of the property (and most likely in the early years while the sinking fund balance is still low) you may also be called upon to contribute a 'special levy'. This levy is usually raised where an item of repair becomes urgent and there is insufficient money in the sinking fund, or where the owners agree on some type of improvement.

When you look to buy property with a body corporate, you must have a good idea of what the levies will be, as well as the current balance of the sinking fund. An older building with a low balance in the sinking fund may spell trouble for you, while a new building with very low contributions may mean that not enough is being put aside for the future.

Don't be lured by low body corporate levies—this is a false economy for you as sooner or later a body corporate with insufficient money in its sinking fund will need to ask the owners for a special contribution. Far better for you to include in your calculations a reasonable levy which will see these things well covered.

Question 12: If it is a Tourism Property, What is the Experience of the Manager and/or the Responsible Entity?

Where the property has any of the management arrangements outlined in Chapter 3, you will want to know what experience the manager has had in managing holiday properties. Where the property is new, you will want a complete history of the other properties that the incoming manager has looked after. Where the property has been in existence for some time, you must ask for historical trading figures.

Where the property is covered by the Managed Investments Act and has a responsible entity, you will also want some information about the experience of this person or organisation. A responsible entity should be able to demonstrate a background of successfully supervising other managed schemes and perhaps even be able to provide testimonials or current client references.

Question 13: Is there a Rent Guarantee?

Where a property is sold with a rent guarantee, you will want to know the terms of this guarantee. In the case of a hotel or resort, sometimes the guarantee is supported by the other income-producing activities undertaken by the hotel. In this case, you will want to know just how this guarantee will be met in times of low occupancy, where there will not be the patrons to spend money on those activities which are meant to support the guarantee.

Where the guarantee is offered personally by the developer or manager, check to ensure that they really have the financial backing to support this. You will want to see annual financial statements and know about their own liquidity position.

In rare cases the rent guarantee is a pool of money provided at settlement of your property, designed to 'top up' rent to an agreed percentage in lean times and last a set period of time. This may be a viable guarantee if the funds have come from developer profit and are actually enough to support the property—that is, do not rely on a fairly high occupancy in the first place. I have seen properties where the rent guarantee is provided as a pool which comes from an increase to the price paid in the first place, with the extra amount providing the guarantee. Where this has not resulted in a purchase price higher than valuation it could be a viable way to obtain a guarantee. Where it has simply added to what you must pay without a resulting benefit (for example, a higher rent return) this is not a true rent guarantee at all.

Now You Are Ready to Make Your Offer

Note that the one thing the questions above have in common is that *none* of them relate to the colour of the kitchen, the views, or how you may personally feel about the property itself. Each question is designed to glean very important information, yet none of them will allow you to become emotionally involved.

I had a client who bought a property from our register. She really wanted to see the property but it was too far for her to travel, so we asked for the agent to send up some pictures. While completing the due diligence, and because of holidays by the client, etc. time passed and soon it was two months since the client had first become interested. When we contacted the agent to say that the client was finally ready to sign contracts the agent apologised, saying that they had sold the property the day before.

> ...one thing the questions have in common is that *none* of them relate to...how you may personally feel about the property itself...

My client was devastated. "Don't worry too much," I told her "There are a lot of very similar properties in the same area, and now that we have completed the research you really only need to pick one." "But I wanted *that* one," she said. When I asked her why, she could not really explain. "It seemed so *good*," was her only reply.

I was able to explain to this client that the reasons for this property seeming so good were all things which would apply to any one of the other properties in the area. I reminded her that this was a business transaction and that she had lost nothing.

Once the research is in place, you are ready to proceed on to making the offer and completing your purchase. Chapter 7 will outline for you the process you will now take in order to make this purchase, no matter which state you live in.

If You Really Must Go and Look

If you are buying a property close by, or you feel the need to take a look at a potential purchase, here are some things to look for while you are there:

Inside the House

- Look for signs of rising damp.
- Assess whether doors and windows are square.
- Check for wall or ceiling cracks. Slight vertical wall cracks are normal but large horizontal cracks may be a problem.
- Test water pressure in taps.
- Fill the bath or sink and check drainage.
- Observe any musty odours which could indicate a moisture problem.

Outside the House

- Inspect gates and fences for rot.
- Check for adequate sub floor ventilation.
- Look at the roof for broken tiles or damaged tin.
- Check the condition of gutters.
- Check stumps for subsidence, rot, or termites.

☞ Look in the back yard for signs that water is not running off adequately.

All of these things will be picked up by a building inspector, but they may be enough to prevent you from going any further and so spending money. Once again, just because these things check out fine, don't go falling in love with the property!

Conclusion

Buying your first investment property is a daunting task. When I purchased my first one, it seemed to take weeks and I panicked about having to effectively 'double' my debt.

Now I am very proficient, and I stick to the process outlined in this chapter, to be sure that my emotions never lead me into making bad decisions. I realise that my discomfort with debt is fine where it relates to personal debt, but unfounded when it comes to securing my future. It is important that we use every resource available to us to ensure that we make the best attempt to secure our future.

7

Buying That Property!

- ➠ **The states all have different rules for purchasing property.**

- ➠ **You should have a good understanding of the similarities and differences between states.**

- ➠ **What a conveyancer or solicitor will do depends on which state you are in.**

CLIENTS OF MINE ONCE lost a sale on an interstate property because they had taken too long to read the contracts. They thought they were safe as they had made an offer which had been accepted by the vendor. Having received the contracts, they assumed that, until they rejected the terms of the contract or otherwise contacted the vendor, the property would still be theirs. When they were ready to accept it was too late, someone else had beaten them to it and the vendor (or the agent) had not even contacted my clients to see if they were going to sign or not.

Although it would have been nice from an ethical point of view for the vendor to make a phone call to my clients, legally he was not required to.

Once you have made the decision to accept only positive cash flow property as an investment, it is likely that your search for property may take you out of your home state. If this is the case, then you must be aware that every state has a different legal system governing how property is transferred from one party to another. Being aware of the differences may save you becoming too disappointed at a later date.

The Point

This chapter will attempt to outline, in a nutshell, the different rules for each state in Australia when purchasing property. Note that this information will not be exhaustive—my research has led me to believe that I would need a complete book just to explain real estate contracts! However, the information here should give you a good starting point.

Negotiating the Price

From the very first point of negotiation, we see marked differences in the way this process is handled in each state. As a general rule, however, it's a bit like a game of cat and mouse where the victor enjoys the spoils. The aim is to try to find the lowest price the vendor is willing to accept. This, of course, is not as easy as it sounds, as he or she is not about to reveal this to you, nor is the selling agent.

In my experience, the purchaser, in most cases, pays more than the bottom dollar that the vendor would have been willing to accept. This is clear if you have ever watched one of the property shows on television—mostly, the vendors have revealed to the cameras beforehand a price they would accept, and the buyers will often pay more than this. We can blame this phenomenon on those old emotions, which make buyers pay too much for a property they have fallen in love with, and vendors hold out for a higher price as they probably believe their property is worth more than it is.

> ... it's a bit like a game of cat and mouse where the victor enjoys the spoils.

Since you have cleverly decided not to let your emotions get the better of you with your investment purchase, you are going to be in the box position. You have time up your sleeve and hundreds of other properties which could do the job for you equally as well as the one on which you are negotiating.

An important issue to raise here is the role of the real estate agent. Be aware that no matter how nice an agent may seem, he or she is working to get as much money for the vendor as possible.

Remember, an agent's commission is a percentage of the actual selling price.

I sold a house of which I owned 50%, along with my parents. It went on the market and less than a week later we had an offer. At first, we had believed that the price would be $300,000 (and so we priced it at $310,000), but the day before this offer came in I called the agent to say that I thought it may fetch more, and that I would like the price raised to $320,000. He was reluctant and suggested that I was asking too much, but I was insistent.

The following day while I was at lunch with a colleague, the agent phoned with an offer—$310,000! Straight away I knew my instincts had been correct (in fact I started to think that I should have gone even higher). The agent was suggesting that I take this offer as this was a genuine, final offer and the buyer had no more money. "I want $320,000," I said, knowing that we had only been on the market for less than a week and we had plenty of time yet. "You will lose the buyer," was the advice, and I told the agent I was prepared for this eventuality (we *did* want to sell the property, but I could not let the agent know this). Fifteen minutes later my phone rang again (my lunch was going cold!): "They've offered $315,000, but they really cannot go any higher," said the agent. "Then they won't be buying my property. The price is $320,000," I said with all the savoir-faire I could manage (secretly cringing at what my parents would do to me if I lost this sale, which had already gone $15,000 higher than they wanted!). He sighed and went away. Ten minutes later (and by now my appetite was completely gone), guess what! Of course we got the $320,000.

The purpose of this illustration is to show you that whoever is toughest wins! As a buyer of property, my suggestion is 'always go in low and then go slow'. You have no reason to rush. In doing so you will get some feeling for how much the vendor is prepared to move. Sometimes it is good to have a few properties being negotiated at the one time—and to be sure your agent knows this. Have firmly in mind the top price that you think the property is worth, and at which you can be sure to get a reasonable cash flow. And remember that, should you exceed this price, you will pay too much and possibly lose that cash flow.

If you cannot get the vendor to agree to your price, then walk away and feign disinterest in going any further with this purchase. The wait may be painful but, if you are sure of your figures, it is likely that after waiting a few days or even a week, the vendor will come back and accept your offer. And, if not, move on to the next property. As I write this book I am waiting on an offer I made one month ago on a commercial property—the vendor wants far more than it is truly worth and I am sure that I am pretty much on the money. If I miss out, no problem—there are a lot more fish in that sea!

Closing the Sale

Once the price is agreed, each state will have it's own requirements for preparing and signing your purchase contracts. It is useful for you to have a good understanding of the similarities and differences between states.

New South Wales

Before placing your property on the market in NSW, the Contract of Sale must be prepared, as this is a state legal requirement. This is because the contract contains all of the relevant disclosure statements—that is declarations identifying pertinent facts that a buyer should be aware of when looking to buy any property.

Once you have agreed on the price, your copy of this contract will be sent over to your solicitor, who will read it and explain it to you.

At this point you will be ordering a pest inspection, a building inspection and your bank may be ordering a valuation, depending on their internal policy and the loan-to-valuation ratio you are seeking (see Chapter 9). These inspections will assist you to further determine the condition of the property, and the valuation may help you establish if the price is right.

Once these tasks are completed, you are ready to 'exchange' contracts. This is the process where the solicitors (or their law clerks) representing each party meet, and 'swap' the contracts, with the purchaser paying a deposit, which is almost always 10% of the price (although you can ask the vendor to take less than this, and they may agree). Up until exchange is effected, the vendor can sell the property to anyone else, for any price they wish. This can make things a little difficult for you, as perusing the contracts and having the required inspections done can take time, sometimes up to and in excess of two weeks. When the vendor sells a property to another party after agreeing to sell it to you, you have been 'gazumped'.

There are two ways that you can avoid being gazumped. Firstly, you can exchange contracts without having any inspections done. This would be recommended only where a property is brand new, and you can be sure that the building is sound. You would also need evidence that a termite treatment had been carried out. The second way to avoid being gazumped is to sign your contracts 'on a 0.25%'. This is real estate speak for signing a contract which prevents the vendor from selling to anyone else, but which will cost you 0.25% of the purchase price if you back out prior to exchange. Depending on the price of the property you are considering, you may see this as a worthwhile option.

> When the vendor sells a property to another party after agreeing to sell it to you, then you have been 'gazumped'.

New South Wales is the most expensive state in which to buy a property in terms of the legal costs involved.

Victoria

The process for Victoria is somewhat similar, with exchange of contracts and a deposit required to secure the property a part of the process. However, there are a few differences.

Once you have narrowed down your search and before you have made any offers, you must be provided with a 'vendor's statement', which is a written statement provided by the seller's legal representative containing a range of information, including:

➩ Seller's details.

➩ Details of easements, covenants and other restrictions on title.

- Zoning details.

- Mortgage details.

- Road access.

- Available services such as water, electricity, etc.

- Outstanding notices such as decisions by councils or roads authorities, etc.

- Building permits issued in the last seven years.

- A copy of the certificate of title.

If you are happy with these disclosures, you are then free to make your offer.

For sale by private treaty (that is, not by auction), your offer will be written into a 'Contract Note' and forwarded, with a deposit, to the vendor. Be aware that a contract note is more than an indication that your offer is serious—it is a legal document and is binding once signed by the vendor.

In some cases, the contract note is the only contract offered. In other cases, an actual contract of sale is subsequently prepared, however if there are general conditions in this subsequent contract with which you are not happy, this is too bad. Signing a contract note means you are agreeing to any general conditions which may be in the contract for sale. General conditions include:

- A provision for the buyer to pay by cash or bank cheque.

- A statement that the buyer has 21 days to arrange 'Requisitions on Title'.

- The rate of interest payable should settlement be delayed.

- A statement that the vendor has an obligation to provide a 'good title'.

A contract note can be 'subject to' conditions—that is it can list a range of conditions which must be satisfied to make the contract binding, such as obtaining finance, or satisfactory inspections. This means that you can go ahead and sign a contract note, stating specific special conditions, and be confident that you have secured the property, even before you have finance in place.

Australian Capital Territory

Again the process is quite similar, with contract exchange required. All offers made, however, are verbal and the law requires that any offer, no matter how far from the ballpark it is, be presented to the vendor. Once an agreement on price has been reached, instructions are sent to the solicitor to prepare the contracts, which can take about ten days. Until exchange occurs, the vendor is free to accept higher offers, and there is no 'cooling off' period available (see page 104). Once again, purchasers are highly vulnerable to gazumping, and with preparation of contracts delayed until after the offer is accepted, this increases the plausible timeframe within which a contract may be exchanged.

Northern Territory

Negotiations are undertaken verbally, but once an agreement is reached on the price, both parties must sign an 'offer to purchase'. This is not a legal document—rather an agreement to the price. Once again, the purchaser is not protected until exchange takes place, and the vendor is free to accept other offers at any time during the lead up to exchange.

South Australia

Once you have made what is considered a reasonable offer to the vendor's agent, he or she will prepare a contract, which includes special conditions (such as a finance clause, etc.). The contract will also outline the deposit payable and the settlement date. Once you have signed, it becomes binding if accepted by the vendor. Cooling off applies in South Australia

Western Australia

Western Australia is one of the easiest states in which to buy and sell property, as you are able to lock in a property fairly simply and do not run the risk of being gazumped.

Once you have chosen the property you wish to negotiate upon, your offer is drawn up on an 'offer and acceptance' form. This form is fairly basic (being just two pages), and lists the offer price as well as any special conditions you would like included. For example, if you have not yet sold the house in which you live, you can ask for a condition making the purchase 'subject to the sale of my own home for at least $200,000'. Note the specifics of the condition are very important—stating just 'subject to selling my home' may not be specific enough if you subsequently do not raise enough from the sale to buy the new property.

You can include any conditions you like. It is up to the vendor to accept both your price *and* your conditions. Your offer and acceptance form will be taken over to the vendor who will read it and either agree, disagree, or perhaps agree with parts of it. For example, the vendor may accept the conditions but not the price. In this case the vendor would cross out your price and write a counter offer for presenting to you. This form then goes back and forth until both parties have agreed, at which time the form is signed and said to be 'accepted'.

An offer and acceptance is a legally binding document, and once it becomes unconditional (that is, all of the conditions have been satisfied) it cannot be revoked. In fact, this offer and acceptance only becomes invalid if the conditions cannot be met in the timeframe allowed, or at all. The vendor cannot sell to anyone else and the buyer cannot back out.

Queensland

Just when you thought you were beginning to see a pattern emerging, let me introduce you to Queensland!

Once you find the property you like, you must request a PAMD (Property and Motor Dealers) Form 27a from the seller's agent. Don't you just love these technical names? This form is a disclosure to the buyer disclosing all material interests and relationships which the selling agent has in the sale. You also need to obtain a PAMD Form 30a, which is a warning statement from the selling agent drawing your attention to items which are important to the contract itself, such as cooling off periods, etc.

If you are happy with these disclosures, you may then make your offer. You sign the Contract of Sale and note any special conditions, such as 'subject to pest and building inspections'. A deposit must accompany the offer.

If your offer is accepted then the agent must arrange the signing by both the buyer and the seller of a PAMD Form 31a, which is a declaration by the seller to let the buyer know when the contract was signed. The buyer then has a cooling off period from this date, unless this has been waived by signing a PAMD Form 32a Lawyers Certification!

If you get through all of this, then you have a binding contract and you can proceed to settlement.

Tasmania

Not only does Tasmania have one of the least complicated systems, it also is one of the cheapest states in which to buy property from a legal cost point of view (most probably because of this simplicity).

Once you have found the right property, you negotiate through the selling agent. The offer is made on a standard Contract of Sale and once accepted by the vendor becomes binding. Like in Western Australia, it can have conditions, which can mean that a contract 'falls over' if any of the conditions are not met. In all states where there is not a separate document with vendor's disclosure statements, material information must be contained in this Contract of Sale.

There is no such thing as gazumping in Tasmania—once the offer is accepted the vendor can not entertain offers from any other party.

Cooling Off

New South Wales, South Australia, Victoria, Queensland and Northern Territory all have what is known as a 'cooling off' period.

This is the right to get out of a contract, providing:

- You notify the vendor in writing within the cooling off period (usually two to five days, depending on the state).

- It is a private sale (not an auction).

- It is a domestic property.

In Victoria, the property also has to have a value of less than $250,000. This does not apply in other states. Tasmania, Western Australia and the ACT have no cooling off provisions.

To cancel a contract you must write to the seller or their agent. You can ask for a full refund of your deposit, although the seller has the right to retain a portion of the deposit paid, usually around 0.25% of the purchase price.

In all states with cooling off, you can waive your cooling off period. This is no great benefit to either party, except that it may make a useful negotiation tool if you have a keen vendor. You may be able to make a slightly lower offer in exchange for waiving the cooling off period. Be very sure that you will not want to change your mind if this is what you decide to do.

Who Does The Legal Work For You?

This depends entirely on the state. New South Wales, South Australia and Northern Territory all allow for 'non-lawyer' conveyancers to carry out property transfers, with each state providing its own legislation to cover this. This means that you have the choice between using a solicitor (property lawyer) or a licensed conveyancer or settlement agent. While Tasmania, Queensland and the ACT have no provision for using a conveyancer (this is being reviewed in Tasmania), in Western Australia 'settlement agents' (conveyancers) are licensed under state law, and are far more popular than solicitors. Although the Legal Practice Act 1996 (Vic) prohibits persons who are not legal practitioners from preparing legal documents relating to land transfers, about 10% of residential conveyancing in Victoria is done by conveyancers who retain lawyers to carry out the legal work, while they perform non-legal tasks such as searches and liaising with the mortgagee.

It will be your choice—some settlement agents and conveyancers offer value for money (with the basic fees usually being less than those of many lawyers). But where there may be an out-of-the-ordinary transaction (say a serviced apartment or some other more complicated structure) you may be better served with a solicitor who can also provide you with valuable legal advice at the same time.

> Some states allow 'do-it-yourself' conveyancing.

Some states allow 'do-it-yourself' conveyancing. My brother did this once, in order to save a little money. I say *once* because, despite having bought a few properties since then, he has never done it again! This speaks volumes about the ease of do-it-yourself conveyancing—and as an investor you have far better things to do just to save a few dollars (which after tax breaks will be a few less dollars anyway!).

What Do They Do?

What a conveyancer or solicitor will do, of course, depends on which state you are in. Generally speaking, however, they will complete the following tasks.

Prepare the Contracts

The Contract of Sale is usually a standard document with provision for additions to be made by the vendor. In some states, the Contract of Sale will contain vendor's disclosures, while in other states these disclosures are made by separate document and prior to the Contract of Sale stage.

Carry Out Searches

Prior to exchanging a contract, the conveyancer will carry out searches to be sure that the title is 'clear' and that there are no encumbrances or other issues which may impede the purchase. This includes searching the title itself, as well as the local council or other government agencies to be sure that there is no planning which will ultimately affect the purchase. These searches must be done before a contract becomes unconditional as searches which turn up issues for which you are not prepared are not cause for cancelling an unconditional contract (unless the condition was that the searches come up clear!).

The Body Corporate Search

If the property you are buying is strata titled, it will have a body corporate. Put simply, a body corporate is a committee of elected people (usually owners or their proxies) whose job is to raise levies in order to ensure that common property is cared for. They will also maintain a sinking fund to pay for future major repairs.

When you buy a strata titled property, it is vital to have a body corporate search carried out. This is not always suggested by conveyancers, so you must ask for this to be done. Most states have an organisation which, for a reasonable fee, will carry out this search for you.

Potential problems can include past or current disputes between owners and the body corporate, or even litigation with the builder for building defects. You will also want to know the state of the sinking fund. A low balance in a sinking fund in an old building could mean that you are shortly to be called upon to contribute to a costly repair. A full search of the body corporate will ensure that you do not find any nasty surprises lurking after settlement.

Exchange the Contracts

Where this is a requirement exchange is attended to by the conveyancer. It is a simple process of meeting with the 'other side' and swapping contracts. Once this is done, the contract is binding unless an event occurs negating the contract, which both parties had agreed to as a condition of sale.

Where no Exchange is Required – Checking Special Conditions

In states where exchange is not required, the conveyancer must help the purchaser meet the special conditions within the timeframe allowed to be sure that the contract does not 'fall over'. Generally a contract with a time period in which to satisfy conditions can be extended if all parties agree.

Carry out the 'Requisitions on Title'

These are questions which your conveyancer will ask the vendor about the property. Generally there will be a timeframe in which you can carry out these requisitions, usually 21 days. There are forms which set out standard questions which are usually used, but be warned—these forms are like *War and Peace* and include many questions which are just not applicable. Vendors are required to read the requisitions and answer each question to the best of their knowledge.

Prepare All Title Transfer Documents

One of my clients bought a property once and sold it eight months later. At that time he discovered that, although his solicitor had prepared a title transfer document, it had never been lodged with the land titles office! The only way he found this out was at this point of sale.

Title transfer documents ensure that legal title to the property is transferred to you, and notifies the land titles office that you are now the legal owner. It must be lodged on settlement of your property, so you may wish to ask for evidence of this after settlement.

Arrange Settlement

This involves ensuring that the vendor's conveyancer is available at the same time that your conveyancer is, and that any lenders involved (vendor and purchaser) have provided the details to release (vendor) and establish (purchaser) the mortgage and the title. This must all take place on the same day (the same minute!).

At the same time (or just before) stamp duty on the purchase must be paid. Many conveyancers will ask for a cheque for the full amount of stamp duty some time prior to settlement day but for many purchasers (particularly investors using home equity as a deposit) this is simply not possible. Don't let your conveyancer tell you that stamp duty *must* be paid before settlement. It can all be done concurrently and you can use the loan funds advanced on the day to pay this—it's just a little more inconvenient for your conveyancer.

Lastly, the conveyancer must calculate adjustments to be made on the day of settlement. For example, if the vendor is ahead with rate payments, then an adjustment will come from proceeds for your portion of these rates, and so on for any costs associated with owning the property.

Contracts will have included a latest date for settlement, after which penalty interest will apply if the property has not settled. Ultimately, meeting this date is your responsibility, not your conveyancer's, so be sure to keep in contact with your legal representative so that this can happen.

Advise Authorities of Sale

Local authorities such as council and water boards will need to be advised by your conveyancer that the transfer has taken place. This is a task for your conveyancer but, once again, do check that it has been completed.

Acquit the Purchase to You

All conveyancers must provide a 'settlement statement'—that is an acquittal of how the funds were distributed and to whom. Keep this statement. It will be needed when you claim your tax deductions, or when you complete your 'Request to Vary Taxation' certificate (see Chapter 10).

What Will it Cost You?

Yet again, the costs of buying a property do vary in each state. This is because, not only do conveyancers have a

> ...the costs of buying a property do vary in each state.

different schedule of fees, each state has different requirements regarding the searches required, and each 'authority' will also have different charges.

In general, you can expect at the very least to pay:

➥ Stamp duty on the purchase, at varying rates according to the state.

- Stamp duty on the mortgage, again at varying rates.

- Land Titles Office registration fees.

- Conveyancing charges.

- Adjustment of rates and taxes.

- Bank establishment fees for any loan.

- Search fees and disbursements.

In addition to this, you may have other costs, such as:

- Accountancy charges.

- Bank cheque fees for settlement.

- Agency fees if you are using a solicitor in your state for a purchase in another (as your solicitor will need to retain an agent to handle the settlement).

- Mine subsidence certificates if you live in a mine subsidence area.

- Building and pest inspection fees.

- Body corporate search fees.

The above list is by no means exhaustive—be guided by your conveyancer, who should be able to advise you on a fairly close estimate of costs.

Auctions

Auctions will progress in the manner above *after* a contract becomes exchanged or unconditional. The process for getting to this stage is a little different, however.

When you choose to bid for a property at an auction, you must be prepared. I do not recommend auctions for people seeking a property as an investment simply because it is too easy to be carried away by the emotion of the day. I laugh when I see the auction shows on TV. In over 90% of the auctions they film, the final bid is considerably above the reserve, and usually made by someone who swore not five minutes before that they had an upper limit which they would stick to (and which they did not).

You cannot just turn up at an auction, successfully bid for a property, and then decline to proceed when you find out things about the property which you may not like. Once your bid is accepted as the final bid and the property is sold to you, you must pay the 10% deposit and sign a binding contract. There is no cooling off period when you buy at auction.

So, it is important for you to carry out the necessary research before auction day, and you must have finance approval in place before bidding. This will mean reviewing the contract, and perhaps even paying for a building and pest inspection beforehand. The problem here of course is that, having paid for these inspections (probably over $500), you may feel a need to press on until you have the winning bid, and this may well result in you paying much more than you intended. This is fine if the cash flow remains positive, but this will rarely be the case. Far better to have more control over the purchase process by leaving auctions to owner occupiers, unless you are truly confident that the property is right for you.

> There is no cooling off period when you buy at auction.

Private Sales

On rare occasions, you may come across a property which is being offered as a private sale. This can be advantageous to both the buyer and the seller as usually a more favourable price for both can be reached without the need to pay out expensive agents' costs.

While a seller does not get the exposure needed to make a quick sale, as a buyer, there is no drawback to buying at a private sale. The same legal pathway must be taken by the vendor even where no seller's agent exists, and the price may well be more negotiable where a middleman is not involved.

Not Negotiable Property

There is no such thing as not negotiable property! All property has a negotiable price. In the case of new property, where there exist sufficient buyers who are willing to pay the asking price, you may not get the opportunity to negotiate. However, where you see property which is available, you are free to make an offer. And, having worked closely with developers in the past I can tell you that you may well find that you can bring the price of even a new property down by a few thousand if you give it a try.

Paying the Deposit

Payment of a 'holding deposit' takes place once the vendor accepts your offer. While there is no legal requirement for a holding deposit, it is usually a sign of good faith and shows the vendor that you are serious. Holding deposits are usually small amounts—a few hundred or perhaps a thousand dollars.

Once a contract becomes exchanged, or unconditional, there is usually a requirement to pay 10% as a deposit, unless you have negotiated a lower amount. This money is then kept in the trust account of either the agent effecting the sale or the solicitor acting on the seller's behalf. If for some reason you do not subsequently proceed with the sale after reaching this point, the 10% deposit is forfeited to the vendor.

But, what if you are using the equity in your own home to form the deposit on the property? I don't know about you but I usually do not have a cool $20,000 or so lying about in my bank account!

Some lenders will allow you an advance on your approved loan, but often this is not possible. This is why 'deposit bonds' are becoming much more popular today than ever before.

What is a Deposit Bond?

A deposit bond is an insurance policy whereby an insurance company guarantees to the vendor that, should you renege on the purchase and not settle (once you have an unconditional or exchanged contract) they will pay the 10% deposit, which is forfeited to the vendor. It does not relieve you of your responsibilities though—as soon as it is paid the insurance company will sue you to recover the money.

An insurance company deposit bond can be a useful and inexpensive tool in your investment strategy. Let's look at the following illustration.

> Marie and George are friends who each buy a one-bedroom apartment as an investment. The price of each apartment is $120,000, and there is a long settlement period—six months.
>
> Marie has a line of credit on her own home with some equity available, so she draws her $12,000 deposit from here (in effect, this $12,000 becomes loan funds, as she will pay interest on the drawings at 6.25%). George, on the other hand, pays $124 to buy a $12,000 deposit bond, with a term of six months.

Their positions are as follows:

- Marie pays $375 interest on her borrowed deposit.
- George has paid only $124 for his bond.
- Both items are tax deductible.

Purchasers in many states are unfamiliar with deposit bonds and those in some states do not need them at all, as a substantial deposit is not required (for example, in WA). Be careful of property 'experts' who advise the indiscriminate use of bonds—look to Chapter 12 for some warnings on the almost illegal use of this tool.

> An insurance company deposit bond can be a useful and inexpensive tool in your investment strategy.

All Settled!

Now that your property is settled, it is time to get it tenanted (see Chapter 8) and get your financial affairs in order (See Chapters 10 and 11). Apart from the fact that the tax department requires your property to be income-producing in order for you to claim a tax deduction, you certainly do not want to start out with a period of vacancy. There is still a lot of work to be done.

Summary

If you are planning on perhaps buying property from many states, the following table is a quick ready reckoner to refer to.

Item	NSW	WA	ACT	VIC	NT	SA	QLD	TAS
Offer & acceptance	No	Yes	No	Contract Note	Yes	No	Yes	No
Separate vendor's statement	No	No	No	Yes	No	No	Yes	No
Offer contract final	No	Yes	No	No	No	Yes	Yes	Yes
Special conditions	No	Yes	Yes	Yes	Yes	Yes	Yes	Yes
Exchange required	Yes	No	Yes	Yes	Yes	No	No	No
Cooling off	Yes	No	No	Yes	Yes	Yes	Yes	No
Conveyancers allowed	Yes	Yes	Yes	For non-legal work	Yes	Yes	No	No
Gazumping	Yes	No	Yes	Yes	Yes	No	Yes	No

Conclusion

Just because a property is 'bricks and mortar' does not mean that it will become a sure fire investment. Understanding how the purchasing process operates in every state will help you gain confidence in going outside of your own area to invest. Putting all of your eggs in one basket is no more right with property than it is with any other investment.

Read on to learn more about strategies for dealing with those legendary 'landlord's nightmares'.

8

Landlords, Property Managers and Tenants

➡ **Being aware of your responsibilities as a landlord will help you to run your investment like the business that it truly is.**

➡ **If you would rather use your own time to create more wealth, have a property manager look after your investment for you.**

➡ **Landlord and tenancy arrangements are governed at the state level, so you need to be aware of the differences.**

I ONCE WATCHED ANOTHER story of horror on television involving a landlord who had scored 'nightmare' tenants, who had subsequently made his property unliveable. The story was being recounted by the property's manager (we will call him Frank), who also happened to be the best mate of the landlord James (and the guy who sold him the property). The property had been a negative cash flow investment which James had bought on the advice of his well-meaning accountant (reluctantly it seemed). The poor guy was not only losing money every week, he suddenly found the house empty, and in such a state after just two years of occupancy that it was condemnable, despite being relatively new.

I must say it was the worst case of tenant neglect I had ever witnessed. With rats breeding under the mounds of rubbish in every room, a garage resembling the local tip and rotting food causing the paint to peel, it was enough to send poor Frank running from the premises! The story was a clear deterrent from property investing, with the finale being that James, totally disillusioned, had Frank sell the property for much less than he had paid, and vowed never to invest in property again!

While watching these events unfold, a few questions sprang to mind:

1. What was Frank doing to prevent this happening?
   As the property manager, the tenants' conduct was his responsibility.

2. How come this was only discovered after two years of occupancy? Surely Frank performed an inspection every three months?

3. Why wasn't James advised to insure his property against damage of this kind? His accountant and property manager were both lacking in this duty.

4. How is it that Frank came out of this with two years' management fees and purchase and sale commissions, while James came out with nothing (less than nothing, actually)?

While Frank was doing a good job on camera of being duly sympathetic toward James's plight, I was thinking that he should be running like the wind and looking for a place to hide. It was largely his negligence which put James in this position in the first place!

While we hear and read about stories of this kind all the time, we really must put them into perspective before we use them as an excuse not to choose property. We can hear of as many as a dozen cases of tenant neglect in any one year. If, however, you compare this figure to the hundreds of thousands of rental properties being leased each year, then this reduces your risk of suffering tenant damage to less than 0.1%. Pretty good odds, really!

The Point

The last thing you need is to have a property which adds to your worries. While people tell me that they would rather manage their property themselves, this is an unnecessary burden which actually saves you very little money in the long run. If you want to manage your property as a hobby, perhaps because you are retired with nothing else to do, then go ahead. But, if you would rather use your own time to create more wealth, then this chapter is for you. It will fill you in on all of the things you need to know about being a landlord. Note that once again, landlord and tenancy arrangements are governed at the state level, with each state having its own version of a Residential Tenancy Act. Following is a general guide. You must confirm details in the state where you ultimately buy your property.

Landlord's Insurance

Your very first job after settlement (or even a few days before settlement) is to ensure that your property is adequately insured. Many companies may tell you that their insurance policies are *suitable* for investment properties, but this does not make them landlord's policies.

Landlord's insurance has special inclusions, and is only offered by a very small number of insurers. A landlord's policy will generally have five components.

> Your very first job... is to ensure that your property is adequately insured.

1. Loss of Rent

You can insure your property against loss of rent in the event that your property suffers damage which makes it unable to be tenanted for a period. Note that this provision will not pay your rent if your tenant moves out and you suffer a period of vacancy considered to be a result of the general market. It only covers *loss*—that is rent which is lost due to the damage. You must be careful not to over or under insure—the company will only pay you the amount you actually lose, and you must prove that this amount represents true market rent.

2. Rent Default and Tenant Theft

Where a tenant is in arrears on the rent and subsequently skips out, a landlord's policy will cover the amount of rent in arrears. There will be a maximum amount which can be paid under any one claim, usually around $3,000, or a set period of weeks.

In addition, if anything has been stolen by the tenant, you can claim the cost of replacing the item, with the usual excesses applied.

3. *Damage*

This includes damage done by the tenant which does not occur as a result of normal wear and tear. In other words, that damage done by the tenant which will bring the local newspaper and their cameras out to visit, and which your house and contents insurance does not cover.

4. *Ordinary House and Contents*

The policy will also include a component to cover normal loss to your building or contents through damage or accident, under the same circumstances as the house you live in. Note that if you have no furniture, then the contents may not need insuring, although your fixtures and fittings may. Also, if you buy a strata titled property, the body corporate will already have in place insurance to cover the building. Be sure to thoroughly check this policy, however—it may not cover the fixtures and fittings inside your four walls.

> Landlord's insurance is not expensive...it usually only averages a few hundred dollars per year.

5. *Liability*

Be sure that the policy you are considering includes an amount for public liability, in the event that a tenant (or any visitors) suffers an injury and subsequently sues you for damages.

Landlord's insurance is not expensive—depending on the amount required it usually only averages a few hundred dollars per year. Under no circumstances should you ever try to save a few pennies by refusing this type of insurance. If you include this in your calculations when assessing a property for cash flow you can ensure that your property is covered for loss *and* delivers a positive cash flow.

Property Managers

As mentioned previously, some people choose to manage their own property. If you consider that the average property management fee is 8% and the average rent is $175 a week, then a gross cost of $728 a year (as little as $385 after tax breaks) is a small price to pay to have the property professionally managed.

People have often asked me how to find a good property manager. From their tone of voice, I gather that they are hard to find. I personally have only ever had one problem with a property manager, and this was easy to fix—I terminated our relationship and found another manager! Whether it is only a rumour that many property managers do not do a good job, or fact, once again careful research should minimise your risk in this area.

Finding a Property Manager

If you have purchased your property from a real estate agent, this is as good a place as any to start looking for your property manager. Find out from this manager how many other properties he or she manages, how many staff help to do the job and what the current vacancy rate is.

If you do a few quick calculations, you should be able to work out if this manager is overworked or not. Let's assume that each property needs:

- One inspection every three months (say that's one-and-a-half-hours total, or six hours for the year).
- Thirty minutes a week to collect the rent and handle the paperwork (twenty-six hours a year).
- Three hours every six months to advertise and let the property (six hours a year).
- Thirty minutes a week to answer tenant enquiries (twenty-six hours a year).
- Two hours every six months to arrange any repairs, etc. (four hours a year).

Each property therefore needs 68 hours a year spent on it. If a property manager works 38 hours a week for 52 weeks a year (having someone do the job while he or she is on annual leave), then the maximum number of properties on the books per person should be about 72. As a maximum, I would say that an efficient person could manage 80 properties. A manager with more than this would not have time to carry out all the tasks required to make your property viable.

You may wish to use the property manager who you asked to provide the condition report mentioned in Chapter 6—either way the important point to note is that you should never set and forget. If the property is not being managed as effectively as you would like, if you are not getting inspection reports every three months, or if the vacancy rate seems a little too high, make an immediate change.

Changing Your Property Manager

Changing your property manager is easy. Simply find a new one, and have this person do it for you! You will be required to fax or post a letter to the existing manager advising that you intend to terminate the contract, and asking that the keys be given to the new manager, who will come over and pick them up for you. The new manager will take over the balance of the existing lease, and then prepare a new one once the lease has expired. The new manager will also prepare a new management agreement covering his or her relationship with you.

> ...if the vacancy rate seems a little too high, make an immediate change.

How Will The Property Manager Find Your Tenants?

Usually tenants are found by advertising the property for lease, in local newspapers and perhaps through internal real estate publications. Sometimes, the manager will charge you for this advertising—in other cases the first week's rent is retained by the manager to reimburse these costs. Once again the way in which these costs are charged to you, and at what rate, will be determined by the state in which you are leasing your property.

Upon applying for tenancy, the prospective tenant completes a 'tenancy application form'. Most property managers have access to a 'bad tenant' database, and this is one advantage of using a professional manager over attempting the job yourself. They can also do a credit check to gain some idea of the prospective tenant's credit history. The tenancy application form includes details of referees for the tenant as well as details of previous tenancy arrangements, allowing the manager to check with previous property managers as to the conduct of the tenant.

Where the property to be leased is a commercial one, many real estate agents will use the same form, while others will have a special commercial application which must be completed. Commercial tenants must provide the names and details of at least three entities with which they have had a business relationship as referees.

Tenancy Agreements

A tenancy agreement refers to the lease of a property, and is a legal contract. Tenancy agreements can be verbal, but as a legal arrangement you will be better protected if they are in writing. The terms of a residential lease will be quite different from those of a commercial property.

Residential Leases

A residential lease can be for any term on which the parties agree, but they are usually for at least six months, with the most common period being twelve months. A lease can have no end date—that is they can be on-going, often with a predetermined period of notice required for vacating the premises.

Once a lease has expired, the tenant may be given the option to renew. If the tenant does not want to renew yet is not quite ready to move out, the landlord can provide a 'week to week' arrangement, whereby the lease is renewed each week.

Residential leases are most commonly prepared by the property manager, using a standard residential lease form (which is particular to each state).

Commercial Leases

A commercial lease is a much more complex document, and is almost always prepared by a solicitor, with the cost of this borne by the tenant.

Prior to the preparation of this lease, the tenant and the landlord will usually negotiate terms, through the property manager. Depending on the location of the commercial property and the demand for it, the landlord may have to offer incentives to attract a tenant.

For example, my business Destiny Financial Solutions recently looked for larger premises. We came across an old building which had a few vacant 'shops', all of which needed a considerable amount of work (having been an old pottery store and, before that, a very old 'general store').

We decided we could make it suitable, and asked the landlord for:

1. Three months free rent so we could renovate.

2. The interior and the exterior to be painted at his cost and effort.

3. The rights to the side wall for signage.

4. A $100 reduction in the monthly rent.

He agreed on the free rent and the side wall for signage, but he would only pay for paint for the outside wall, so we had to paint the wall and pay for and arrange the internal painting ourselves. We also did not get a reduction in the rent amount.

Incentives can include assistance with the fit-out, rent-free periods, rent reductions, etc. Tenancy arrangements are usually for a minimum of two years (although with high vacancy rates tenants can often negotiate shorter periods), and the landlord is usually required to provide an option to extend for another two years (or whatever the agreed period is). This is because it would not do to pay out a substantial sum of money renovating premises and establishing a business if you could not have some assurance that you could maintain your residency for a reasonable period of time.

Bonds

A bond is a sum of money paid by the tenant, and held by the respective states' Bond Authority. It is usually an amount equivalent to four weeks rent. The purpose of a bond is to meet the cost of any repairs required after the tenant has vacated. A bond is not for attending to 'normal wear and tear' such as carpet cleaning or garden maintenance. It can only be used if the tenant has been negligent and caused damage to your property. Once the tenant has vacated the property, you must carry out an inspection and return the bond (or what remains of the bond) to the tenant at your earliest convenience.

Condition Report

Prior to a new tenant taking up residency, you or your property manager must complete a condition report. This report must be given to your tenant in duplicate at the start of the tenancy. They must check the report, make any alterations they see fit, sign both copies and return it within three business days of moving in. The report will then be the basis for refunding the bond at the end of the tenancy period.

Rent

Tenants have a legal obligation to pay rent and to continue to pay rent until the end of the tenancy period. Residential rent is usually payable at least one week in advance, while commercial rent is usually payable one month in advance.

There are limits on how much rent in advance you can demand. For rent payable weekly, you can only ask for two weeks in advance. For rent payable more than weekly, you cannot demand any more than one month's rent in advance.

The person receiving the rent must issue a receipt for the rent collected.

Where the term of the lease is fixed, residential rents cannot be increased during that fixed term unless the lease has a clause which relates to rent increases. Laws in some states require as much as

90 days notice for a rent increase, and this notice must be given in writing.

A commercial lease will generally have written into it a clause which states that rent will increase each year, most commonly in line with the Consumer Price Index (inflation rate).

Where a tenant is in arrears with rent, you (or your property manager) must contact him or her to see if an arrangement can be reached to rectify this situation. If this is not possible, then you may give the tenant notice to vacate the premises. It is illegal for a landlord to change the locks or otherwise 'lock out' a tenant, or try to physically evict the tenant. It is important to note that while we do hear reports of landlords unable to evict tenants who refuse to pay rent, thankfully these cases are rare and should not become one of your reasons not to invest in property.

Ending a Tenancy Early

Your tenant cannot just walk out in the middle of a lease. However, if you both agree then a lease can be broken early.

If a tenant does walk out and stop payments, some states have an arrangement whereby you can apply to be compensated for any money lost as a result of this breach of lease—such as lost rent, advertising costs for a new tenant and any re-letting fee.

As a landlord, you have a legal obligation to provide safe premises for your tenants.

Where completing a tenancy arrangement may cause hardship for the tenant, some state tenancy authorities may allow the tenant to break a lease.

Landlord Responsibilities

As a landlord, you have a legal obligation to provide safe premises for your tenants. Your tenant has the right to expect peace, privacy and quiet. A lease gives you no protection from contingent liability to your tenant while he or she is in residence.

In order to fulfil your obligations to the tenant you must:

➥ Have the premises inspected regularly.

➥ Check the structure, pipes, water heater, etc.

➥ Have a public risk policy.

➥ Have the property inspected by a building inspector before purchasing to be sure that it is safe to inhabit.

There have been recent cases where injury and theft were deemed to be the result of a landlord failing in his or her duty of care to provide a safe place, and the landlord has been ordered to pay compensation to the tenants, even where a third party caused the loss!

Repairs

If tenants have caused damage to your property, you are entitled to ask them to pay for its repair. If the damage is not the fault of the tenants, then you are liable for it and must have it repaired as soon as possible.

Urgent repairs must be attended to immediately, and include:

➥ Blocked lavatories.

➥ Flood damage.

➥ Gas leaks.

➥ Roof leaks.

➥ Burst hot water service.

➥ Breakdown of an essential service or appliance.

➥ Storm or fire damage.

➥ Any fault making the premises unsafe.

➥ A serious fault in a lift or staircase.

Where a repair is urgent, tenants must make a reasonable effort to contact either you or the property manager. If they are unable to do so, they may organise repairs up to $1,000. You must then reimburse the tenant within 14 days.

Where a repair is not urgent, or caused by normal wear and tear, tenants must ask you to arrange these repairs. Generally, you will have 14 days to do so.

Costs You May Not Expect

As a landlord, you probably expect to pay the rates, the body corporate levies (if any), repairs and property management fees. You will also have insurance to pay, and interest on any loans used to make the purchase.

There are also some other costs which many investors do not anticipate. While you may never incur these costs, it is helpful to know what they are so that you may include them in your calculations for cash flow if you believe they might be incurred.

Letting Fees

Depending on the state in which you live, you may have to pay a letting fee, most often the equivalent of one week's rent. If your property changes tenants every six months, then this will result in two weeks less rent a year earned by you. In addition to this, some property managers will charge you the costs to advertise for a tenant.

Sundries

Ensure that the property management fee quoted to you includes all sundries and GST. I have seen arrangements whereby the manager quotes a 7.5% management fee, which actually becomes 9.5% once you add the sundry charges and the GST. Ask the manager to quote you a flat rate, and do not be afraid to negotiate this, at least for the first few months of your relationship.

Water Charges

In some states, tenants are responsible for their own water usage. In others, the landlord must pay the rates *and* the usage. If you have a property where this is required, it is useful to consider paying to have 'water saver' shower heads and taps installed.

A little money spent now (tax deductible, of course) may save you a lot of money later.

Cleaning Costs

When your tenant moves out, you may be required to have the carpets and the property professionally cleaned. If you have purchased in another state, you are unlikely to be attending to this yourself. The cost of a professional clean, if you include carpets, can be well over $100. If your tenants change over every six months, then this can once again eat into your cash flow.

Repairs

Choosing a new property does not always mean that you will have no repairs. I had several items requiring repair in the first two years of purchasing one of my new properties. These items were not covered under any building warranty as they were considered normal wear and tear. You must be careful that the property does not have too many 'added extras' which may just contribute to the pool of items requiring repair, such as dishwashers, air conditioners and reticulation systems, all of which add to your potential costs but rarely attract more rent.

Land Tax

Land tax will be covered in more detail in Chapter 10. In a nutshell, once the value of your land holdings (that is the value without the dwelling) exceeds an upper limit (which is particular to each state), then you may be liable for land tax. In NSW all investment property attracts land tax at various rates as well as a duty upon sale. Be sure to check your position on this as it can sometimes be legally avoided if you are careful.

Accounting Fees

At present, you may well complete your own tax return (possibly with some success). Once you have purchased a property, you may want to employ the services of a professional accountant. When you are having a tax return prepared which includes more than just an ordinary salary or wage acquittal, there could be more work involved and therefore more cost. This is an important extra cost to consider which is often overlooked by investors in any type of investment. (For more information on tax see Chapter 10.)

Pest Control

At some time in the future, you may be required to pay for pest control to eradicate ants, cockroaches or even rats and mice. For strata titled properties, this cost may be taken care of from body corporate levies. Some properties may never need professional pest control, and a few cans of a good quality surface spray may do the trick!

Pool and/or Garden Care

Where the property has a pool, you may need a professional to care for this, or at the very least you will need to provide the chemicals if you expect the tenant to keep it clean. Where the gardens are more extensive than a simple lawn and flower bed, you may also want to pay for garden maintenance. I have a very simple and inexpensive way to deal with this issue—I never buy a property with a pool or a landscaped garden, unless it is part of a resort-style investment and therefore professionally maintained.

Travel Costs for Inspections

I have a property which, until last year, I had never seen except for in a photograph. I still have not looked inside, and I trust my property manager, who carries out regular inspections and sends me detailed reports. You may not be as comfortable with leaving your fate to the professionals and may at some time wish to visit the premises and inspect. If you incur travel costs, these may be offset against income as a tax deduction.

I have seen investors buy real estate in popular tourist areas, simply so they can take a holiday twice a year to 'inspect' the property. This is in fact the way many shrewd marketers sell their properties. Make no mistake—tax law is all about 'intent' and if the tax department thinks for one minute that you may have an ulterior motive for having purchased this property (such as to take tax deductible holidays), it will not hesitate to disallow a claim.

Don't let the lure of cheap holidays lead you to make a purchase which may not be right for you in other ways, as this is once again allowing your emotions to muddy the waters. If you do buy property which is far away and you must go and inspect it from time to time, then be sure to factor in these costs when calculating the cash flow.

What Does This All Mean?

Let's translate this into what you should be seeking when considering a property as an investment. Where you are choosing property which has a high turnover of tenants (such as in far North Queensland) be sure that the positive cash flow is considerably higher for your purchase price than you would normally find (as is usually the case in areas such as these). This will then cover any of the extra costs outlined above. If you plan for every reasonable contingency and you are still able to obtain a positive cash flow, then when you don't have to pay out for these unexpected costs, your cash flow will be higher again.

Conclusion

Being aware of your responsibilities as a landlord will help you to run your investment like the business that it truly is. There is no substitute for a good property manager, but having one does not exempt you from your responsibilities or expenses. Take an active (if long distance) interest in what the property manager is doing, and do not hesitate to terminate your relationship with a manager who does not seem to have your best interests at heart.

As you accumulate more properties you will begin to appreciate the true advantages of having help with the management. You will also begin to learn more about choosing a good manager, and find that it is not really so hard after all.

> Don't let the lure of cheap holidays lead you to make a purchase which may not be right for you in other ways...

9 Financing Positive Cash Flow Property

▪▶ A vital aspect of your investment strategy is understanding how different types of loans work.

▪▶ Despite the abundance of options, there are still just a few basic types of loans.

▪▶ The success of your entire portfolio can be enhanced by the careful selection of the right loan product.

IN AUSTRALIA TODAY MORE than 40% of all home loan finance is written on behalf of banks and other lenders by finance brokers. While the laws which govern finance brokers vary from state to state, there is little regulation of the finance broker industry, with most states of Australia requiring no more than a promise of following a code of practice in return for becoming a broker.

While this may have resulted in expanded consumer choice and access to more information, it has also resulted in an abundance of largely unqualified people providing loan advice to borrowers which very often turns out to be inappropriate or simply wrong for the people concerned.

Many finance brokers today choose to supplement their often quite substantial income from their 'loan books' (that is the value of the total loans written by the broker) by teaming up with developers to also offer investors access to property which the investors may otherwise not know about. While this can be beneficial to the investor, all too often the lack of qualifications of the broker results in investors acquiring property which is not necessarily right for their personal financial circumstances. In addition to this, very often the investor has also paid too much for the property (due to the commissions paid to the broker for the sale) and the finance provided has been inappropriate or poorly structured.

Borrowing to invest in real estate is *not* the same as borrowing for real estate in which you would like to live. Your personal 'loan portfolio' must be carefully constructed so that it not only suits your lifestyle today, but remains appropriate to your on-going investment strategy.

The Point

While accountants and financial planners can often provide access to finance for your investment needs, they, like finance brokers, do not necessarily know how to structure a loan portfolio to suit your individual current and on-going needs. A vital aspect of your investment strategy is understanding how different types of loans work, and knowing just what type of loan is right for you.

Borrowing to Invest

In earlier chapters we explored the benefits of borrowing to invest. Using borrowed funds not only allows you to access a greater number of properties, it allows you to increase your exposure to a rising market. If you obtain the right loan, then the amount borrowed will never increase, yet the property you have secured with this money will steadily rise in value over time. Borrowed funds allow you to access capital gains, even if you have no cash of your own.

> Borrowing to invest in real estate is *not* the same as borrowing for real estate in which you would like to live.

We have also covered the fact that positive cash flow property allows you to hedge against a number of the potential pitfalls of investing in property—it can provide a hedge against rising interest rates, decreasing rent returns and an under-supply of tenants.

However, all of this does not mean that any loan will do. Too many people simply look for the lowest interest rate, without realising that these loans often come without the flexibility you need to finalise the loan sooner and so invest again more quickly. The performance of your property portfolio can be further enhanced by choosing your loan carefully in the first place, and then managing it even more carefully from then on.

> When Derek and Fran first came to see me, they already had a property portfolio in place. In addition to their own house, they owned three other properties. To my delight, two of these were positive cash flow (purely by accident, I was assured by them both!). The broker arranging their loan package had put in place an interest-only loan on each of the investment properties, and a principal and interest loan on the house in which they lived.

Now, this may seem like the standard loan set up for investors, and indeed it is. But the problems here were many:

- Fran and Derek had an inflexible loan on their own home, one which did not enable them to use the cash flow from their investment properties to enhance their position on their owner-occupied home.

- The return from each property was attributed to each separate loan. Where the cash flow was positive, the extra funds were spent by Fran and Derek. The negative cash flow property was supplemented by Fran and Derek, using money which may otherwise have gone into the loan on their own home.

- Fran and Derek have four loans where one would do, incurring extra and unnecessary bank fees and charges.

- Both Fran and Derek believed that they were never allowed to pay any extra funds into their interest-only loans as they were 'interest only'. While at this stage in their lives it *is* best to keep them as interest only, as soon as the owner-occupied loan is finalised the best thing for them to do is to pay off their investment debt.

↪ The bank may well hold more security than it actually needs. Since each property is securing one loan, each time that loan was applied for the bank automatically took a mortgage over that property. If Fran and Derek had a high degree of equity in their own home when they started, it could be that only two or three of the properties would be needed to secure the entire debt. It is important that a borrower never give any more security to the bank than is needed.

The salespeople selling the properties to Fran and Derek had used the 'interest-only loan' angle as a selling point, advising Fran and Derek that they need never worry about having to pay off these loans. The broker had benefited from writing so many loans— obtaining 'up front' commissions for each new loan written, when in fact the original loan could easily have just been extended, and none of these 'advisers' had even considered the tax effectiveness of the structure.

Borrowing to invest is a legitimate and potentially very profitable investment strategy *if* you know what you are doing from the outset. While later chapters will deal with tax-effective structures for investing, let us now look at how a bank assesses you for a loan, the different types of loans available, and identify the best way to structure your investment loan portfolio.

Qualifying for a Loan

I have some new clients who, prior to coming to Destiny Financial Solutions, travelled to Brisbane and, at a frightening cost, attended a four-day course which claimed that it would teach them how to acquire millions of dollars worth of property in just a year or two! I admit that the course presenter had some very 'interesting' ideas, but the reality for these (and many other) people was that they were just never going to be able to put these ideas into practice. Not because they were not willing or somehow unable to grasp the concepts—rather because the methods presented to them

> Borrowing to invest is a legitimate... investment strategy *if* you know what you are doing from the outset.

required banks to provide the money. And, no matter how cleverly one can put together a loan application, all banks have lending criteria which will, at some time, place a limit on the amount of money you can borrow.

This is not done because they are mean, or trying to dictate terms. It is a safety mechanism to ensure that their customers do not over-commit and can continue to live a comfortable lifestyle. The last thing a bank needs is to be appearing on a current affairs program because they provided enough credit to over-commit some poor uninformed soul who is now facing financial ruin!

All banks have their own methods for assessing the ability of an applicant to afford the required funds. However there are two basic criteria which all applicants must meet when looking to borrow funds for any purpose.

Equity Criteria

A borrower will need to show that he or she has either sufficient cash, or enough equity in current property holdings, to be able to qualify for the loan.

You may have heard that it is possible to borrow 110% of the value of an investment property (the 10% being provided to pay costs). In fact, this is how many investment properties are marketed. While this may be true, it is misleading, as a lender will not actually give you 110% of any property unless you can provide additional security elsewhere.

Most lenders will provide up to 95% of the market value of an owner-occupied property, and up to 90% of the market value of an investment property. This means that you either need the difference (5% or 10% plus any purchasing costs) in cash, or available as equity in other property you may have. The amount of money you wish to borrow in relation to the value of the security you have to offer is known as the 'loan-to-valuation' ratio.

Where you are borrowing any more than 80% of total market value of your property, the bank will require you to take out a 'lender's mortgage insurance' policy. Later in this chapter is a section dealing with this type of insurance.

As for being able to borrow 110% of the value of a property, it is only where you are using equity in other property as well that you are able to borrow 110% of the purchase price. This is only because you are in fact providing security for more than 110%.

Here's an example:

> Karyn owns a home worth $250,000, on which she owes $50,000. At present, her loan represents 20% of the market value of her home.
>
> She wants to buy an investment property valued at $160,000, so she will need a further $170,000 to make this purchase, which the bank approves.
>
> Now she has a loan which totals $220,000. The bank will need to take the new property as security alongside the one they have. They now hold securities totalling $410,000. Karyn's new loan represents around 54% of the total market value of the securities the bank now holds.

From an *equity* point of view, Karyn could keep adding properties in this way until she reaches the maximum 80% (90% with lender's mortgage insurance), providing she continues to qualify under the *income* criteria.

Had her present home been valued at $275,000, then in fact she would have been able to put in place an additional loan against her own home, without the need to give the bank the title to the new property. Some people feel this gives them a measure of safety as they are then able to hold at least one title unencumbered.

If this were me, I would use as much of the equity as possible, and so buy three investment properties, rather than just one! The point here is to be very careful that the bank does not take security over a property if they don't need to. Just because they are lending you the funds to buy a particular property does not mean they need *that* property to secure those funds.

Income Criteria

In addition to having enough security, a borrower must also have the income required to support the loan. All too often clients have phoned me upset because they own a property worth $800,000 and the bank will not lend them $100,000 because they have no job! Conversely, I have had other people angry because they earn $200,000 a year but, because they have no savings (cannot show the 5% deposit plus costs), the bank will not lend to them.

A lender must be satisfied that, not only do you have the capacity to repay (sufficient income from stable employment), but you also have the capacity to commit the income that you do earn (which having a deposit will clearly demonstrate). A very high income-earner with no savings and no plausible explanation for this clearly has a money management problem!

> In addition to having enough security, a borrower must also have the income required to support the loan.

To calculate a borrower's capacity to repay a loan, a lender will use one of two common methods.

Debt Servicing Ratio

Put simply, a lender using a debt servicing ratio will let you borrow an amount which requires no more than 30% of your gross income per year to repay. Some lenders will go as high as 35%.

> Chris earns $75,000 a year. His bank will let him have a loan which requires no more than $22,500 a year in repayments. If he already has other loans or credit cards, the commitment to them must be deducted from the $22,500 first, and any remaining funds can then be committed to the new loan.
>
> In addition any commitments to child maintenance, store cards, hire purchase, tax debts or any other regular commitment will impact on the amount which can be borrowed.

Each lender will have a different set of rules with regard to the income which is acceptable, but basically they will include:

- Salary and wages from permanent employment.

- A proportion of any existing or expected rental income (usually 80%).

- A proportion of overtime and commissions (usually 50%).

- Business income where the business is well established.

- Depreciation from investment properties or business (this is assessed as income).

- Social security payments (banks have very different rules here).

- Other income where it can be proven.

One of the problems with a debt servicing ratio is that it can over-commit a low-income earner, and limit a high-income earner. A person earning $25,000 a year would be allowed to commit $7,500 a year to loan repayments, leaving only $17,500 to support a family for an entire year and pay tax! On the other hand a person who earns $150,000 a year would be only allowed to commit $45,000 a year to loan repayments, when in fact the high income would mean that this person could actually afford substantially more than this.

It is for this reason that many lenders are now using what is known as a serviceability criteria when assessing applicants for a loan.

Serviceability Criteria

This is a method where the lender takes into account all of an applicant's commitments, including the proposed loan and daily living expenses (for the borrower and his or her family), and allows the applicant to borrow an amount which remains within a certain income/outgo ratio. As an example, ABC Bank may allow its clients to borrow an amount which gives them an income/outgo ratio of no less than 1.10. In laymen's terms, this means that their clients must have as a minimum $1.10 coming in to their household for every $1.00 which is committed. When borrowing to invest, a lender will usually take into consideration the tax advantages afforded by claiming the loan interest, and this can increase borrowing capacity.

All banks using this method will have a different ratio, and it is almost impossible to calculate this on your own, as they have a standard scale of living expenses which they will use.

If you would like to get an idea of your own borrowing capacity, Destiny Finsoft includes a basic calculator (see access details at the back of this book for more information). Do remember that this will be a guide only and your bank may use a different method altogether.

Lender's Mortgage Insurance

Once the loan-to-valuation ratio of your loan exceeds 80% (75% in some cases), the decision to lend to you no longer rests solely with the bank to which you have applied. This is because whenever you borrow greater than 80% of the market value of a property, the bank is taking a larger risk. In the event that you become unable to meet your commitments, and the bank must seize your property for a mortgagee sale, they want to be very sure that they can get enough on the sale to cover what you owe. If not, then lender's mortgage insurance can pay the difference.

> Sam and Anna bought a property worth $180,000. They borrowed $171,000 (95%), having 5% in cash and using the first home owner's grant to pay costs.
>
> The market was high at the time of purchase, but slowed down considerably a short time later, resulting in a stand still. During this time, Sam lost his job. They were unable to meet the loan repayments, and so they got behind and the loan started to go backwards. Eventually, the bank held a mortgagee sale, but not before the loan had reached $179,000.

Due to the downturn in the market, the bank only received $168,000 for the house, and from this incurred $2,500 in selling costs. The bank is now out of pocket by $13,500, which the mortgage insurer then pays.

Note that, had Sam and Anna only borrowed 80% of the market value, even the slowdown in the market would not have affected the bank's ability to recover their funds. This is why lender's mortgage insurance is only applied where the loan-to-valuation ratio is high.

Lender's mortgage insurance is a policy for the bank, but the premium must be paid by the borrower. Since lender's mortgage insurance premiums are high (up to 1.8% of the loan amount, depending on the loan-to-valuation ratio) they can add substantially to your purchasing costs. In addition to this, both the bank and the insurer must approve you for the loan. Where approval is granted by only one, there will be no loan. Since there are only three mortgage insurers in Australia (at the time of writing), if you are declined by one bank because an insurer has rejected you, it is highly likely the next bank will be using the same insurer!

When obtaining a loan requiring mortgage insurance, the insurer will want to see some evidence that you have saved at least some of the deposit on your own.

TYPES OF LOANS

Today there are dozens of different types of loans, with banks attaching all manner of frills to entice you into taking out their product. Gone are the days when borrowers scraped their knees begging to be considered for a loan—consumers now have the choice and banks and other lenders are competing fiercely for their custom.

So, how do we know which loan to take? If we cut through the outer packaging, we will see that despite the abundance of options, there still remain just a few basic choices.

Principal and Interest Loans

A principal and interest (P&I) loan is any loan where an amount is borrowed, and the bank provides a set time in which to repay the entire amount, plus interest. In order to repay the borrowed amount plus the interest within the time period allowed, the borrower will need to make regular payments made up of some of the principal and all of the interest accrued since the last repayment.

When the interest rate rises, so will the amount required as a repayment. This new, higher amount of repayment will not mean that the borrower is repaying more of the principal—it simply means that the interest bill is higher.

Principal and interest loans will usually have a term of somewhere between 25 and 30 years, although you can have a shorter term if you wish (resulting, of course, in a higher repayment). The lender will usually require at least a monthly repayment, although you can often pay with more frequency than this.

The important point to understand about these types of loans is this: although interest is charged back to your loan only once a month, it will accrue on a daily balance. Therefore, those who make a payment fortnightly or weekly will have different (and lower) balances on which interest accrues, while those only making monthly repayments will incur interest on the same balance for the whole month. Let us look at the following illustration.

> Betty owes $100,000 and has an interest rate of 6.25% per annum. She pays $1,000 a month.
>
> After drawing down her $100,000, she is given a repayment date one month hence. So, for 30 days her outstanding balance is $100,000, on which she pays a rate equivalent to 6.25% per annum.
>
> $$\frac{(\$100,000 \times 0.0625)}{365 \text{ days}} \times 30 \text{ days} = \$513.70 \text{ in interest}$$

When Betty pays her $1,000 on day 30, her balance will reduce to $99,000, then immediately increase back to $99,513.70 as soon as the bank adds the interest.

This $99,513.70 will then be accruing interest as above for the next 30 to 31 days.

Helen has the same loan, approved and drawn down on the same day. She decides to take the monthly repayment, but pay it as a weekly instalment. Her weekly payment will be:

$$\frac{(\$1,000 \times 12 \text{ months})}{365 \text{ days}} = \$32.88 \text{ each day } (\$230 \text{ for } 7 \text{ days})$$

The following example shows how Helen's interest accrues. Note that although she pays weekly, the bank does not add the interest to the balance until the last day.

	Balance	Interest accrued	Payment made
Week 1	$100,000	$119.86	$230
Week 2	$99,770	$119.58	$230
Week 3	$99,540	$119.31	$230
Week 4	$99,310	$119.03	$230
Last 2 days	$99,080	$33.93	$80 (notional only)

On day 30, Helen's balance is $99,000, and the bank adds $511.71. She begins the next month with a balance of $99,511.71. Granted, this is only $2 less than Betty, but if you were to look at this over a 25-year period, then the amount of money saved will increase exponentially over this time.

In actual fact, Helen is a little more keen than this. She decides to take the monthly repayment, and divide it by four, paying that amount each week. Let us have a look at the impact of doing this.

	Balance	Interest accrued	Payment made
Week 1	$100,000	$119.86	$250
Week 2	$99,750	$119.56	$250
Week 3	$99,500	$119.26	$250
Week 4	$99,250	$118.96	$250
Last 2 days	$99,000	$33.90	$71 (notional only)

Helen now starts the month with a balance of $98,929, on which the bank adds accrued interest of $511.54, making a total starting balance for month two of $99,440.54.

The point I am trying to make here is this: while the above illustration does show that Helen now starts her month with a loan balance which is $71.17 lower than had she just paid the required amount, only 17¢ of this can be attributed to interest savings. The remainder is a result of extra money paid from Helen's own pocket.

> It is vital that you finalise the loan on your own home as quickly as you can.

How often have you seen advertisements on television which show a young couple gasping in surprise at the difference in their loan term if they make weekly repayments instead of monthly? The advertisements are all about showing how wonderful the bank is, when in reality all that is happening is that you are providing more of your own funds, and this is how the loan term is reduced.

Despite being misled into thinking that this is some kind of bonus being offered to you by the banks, extra repayments to your loans *are* a good thing. It is vital that you finalise the loan on your own home as quickly as you can. The quicker you get equity in your home, the sooner you can begin on the investment plan which will create an income for life! However, do realise that, both for your own home and for your investment portfolio, a principal and interest loan most probably will not provide the true flexibility you need, despite what the bank may lead you to believe about those extra repayments.

'Honeymoon' and Fixed-Rate Loans

The year 2001 brought with it more interest rate cuts than we have ever seen in one year. I personally marvelled at interest rates being offered as low as 3.99%! Add to this free holidays, low or no establishment fees and a host of other 'tempters' and it certainly will go down as the year with more lending opportunities than ever before.

Usually, any incentive will come at some price. There really is no such thing as a free lunch, and so where rewards for borrowing funds are offered, it is more important than ever before that you read the fine print to see what the real 'opportunity' cost may be.

The Honeymoon Rate

A honeymoon rate is simply a low start rate, which can be offered to you as an incentive, usually for a period of 6 to 12 months. Beware the hidden conditions of honeymoon rates—more often than not you will be locked into the loan for a period which may well surpass the actual timeframe of the low rate. For example, a six-month low rate period may come with the condition that you do not pay-out your loan for a further three years.

Be very careful with this one, and don't be too sure that you do intend to stay in the one place as long as these conditions apply. Look back at the past five years of your life—how many changes have occurred which you simply could not have anticipated? Perhaps you moved, changed jobs, got a pay rise or any one of a hundred other things which may have sent you looking for a new home in which to live. If this is you, imagine how those plans would have been ruined if the bank would not allow you to pay-out your loan, or applied a hefty penalty for early pay-out.

Fixed-Rate Loans

A fixed-rate loan is any loan where the rate of interest is set for a pre-agreed term. Over recent years there have been at least four occasions where several of my clients have phoned and asked me if I thought they should fix their loan interest rates. Usually, the query has come in response to a rumour that overseas rates will rise and Australia will follow. On only one occasion did the rates actually rise, and they sharply fell again within two months!

In all of the years I have been practising as a financial adviser I believe I have spoken to less than five people who are truly happy that they fixed their loans. The fear comes when people remember the 1980s, when rates skyrocketed out of control.

> Geoff is a great example. Back when rates were around 7%, he truly believed that they were about to rise. He was offered a three-year fixed rate of 7.3%, which he accepted. Immediately after this, the rates did climb, to 7.5% for two months, and then 7.75% for two months. They peaked at 8%, where they sat for one month, and then dropped over the next six months to below 7%.

In all, there were eight months where Geoff was paying an interest rate less than the variable. For one month, he was paying 0.7% less, for four months he was paying 0.45% less, for two months he was paying 0.2% less and for one month he was paying 0.1% less.

He is still in his fixed-rate term (at the time of writing), and in fact has around 11 months to go. For 16 months, Geoff has paid more than the variable rate. As there is no sign of a rise on the horizon, and with rates well below 6.25%, Geoff has paid out considerably more than he saved. And for all of those who did not fix their interest rates during this time of uncertainty? They have saved considerably more than they paid out. Any one of the people who did wait could have fixed their loans at any time had the trend continued. It is important that you wait until a trend has been established, and remember that the price for fixing a loan may be more than just being stuck with a higher rate, in the event that your circumstances change and you need to get out earlier than expected. Fixed-rate loans can carry very high penalties for early repayment.

Any extra that you may pay by not nabbing that 'fantastic' fixed rate while you could may well be saved by being on what is usually a lower variable rate during that time. You can usually fix most loans at any time, for a fee, but do be aware that the lack of flexibility of a fixed-rate loan may actually slow down your investing, resulting in lost opportunity.

Interest-Only Loans

Interest-only loans became very popular with property traders who wished to buy a property, turn it over in the short term and make a profit without having to invest too much of their own funds.

An interest only loan is any loan where the only repayment required is the accrued interest. This includes lines of credit (although these will be dealt with under a separate section).

These types of loans have become very popular with property investors for one main reason—since most people buy negatively geared property, the less of their own funds they must commit the better. An interest-only loan allows you to keep the loan fully drawn, resulting in a lower monthly repayment, and less money from your

> Interest-only loans became very popular with property traders...

pocket. An interest-only loan usually has a term of five or ten years, at the end of which the borrower must either roll the loan into a principal and interest loan, or renegotiate a new interest-only term (both for a fee, of course!).

When Would I Use this Type of Loan?

Where you still have a debt on your own home, an interest-only loan is a viable choice for investing. This is because interest accruing on an investment loan provides a tax deduction to you, while interest accruing on a property in which you live does not. While you have personal, non–tax-deductible debt and investment, tax-deductible debt, it is obviously desirable to put as much money as you can into the non–tax-deductible debt. You do not want to reduce your tax deductions while you are keeping a non–tax-deductible debt high.

Here's an illustration. For the purposes of this example, I have taken a flat rate of interest over a year, despite the fact that, in reality, the amount of interest paid on all of the loans here would reduce as each repayment reduced the outstanding balance.

> Lesley has a home loan of $100,000, and an investment debt of $150,000 on a positive cash flow property. Both loans are P&I and both are at 6.25% per annum. Her interest bill on the home loan is $6,250 a year, while on her investment debt it is $9,375. Since she earns her personal income in the 30% tax bracket, she can claim a deduction on the loan interest for her investment, in effect giving her back $2,813 of her tax.
>
> Not considering the income on the property or other tax deductions, her position is as follows:
>
> ➠ She owes $100,000 on her home, and $150,000 on her investment, a total of $250,000.
>
> ➠ She pays out $15,625 in loan interest.
>
> ➠ She receives back $2,813 in tax.
>
> ➠ She actually only pays out the equivalent of $12,812 in loan interest.
>
> Let's project this five years down the track.

Lesley has now paid some money off both loans as per her P&I requirement. Let's assume she has paid $20,000 off the home loan, and $30,000 off the investment loan. She is now required to pay $5,000 a year in interest on the home loan and $7,500 on the investment loan. At the 30% rate of tax, she would get back $2,250.

Her position is as follows:

➠ She owes $80,000 on her home and $120,000 on her investment, a total of $200,000.

➠ She pays out $12,500 in total loan interest.

➠ She receives back $2,250 in tax.

➠ She actually only pays out the equivalent of $10,250 in loan interest.

It all looks good as the loans are reducing and she is getting equity in her loan portfolio. Not taking into account the natural market value increase in both her properties, Lesley now owns $50,000 more of her portfolio, and has had tax refunded over these five years of more than $13,000.

But wait! There is a better way!

Imagine that Lesley chose an interest-only loan as her investment loan. The year one figures in this illustration would remain the same, but what would happen in year five?

Lesley would still have paid the $50,000 in total off her portfolio, but since the investment loan is interest only, she would have directed all of these funds to just her personal debt, leaving the investment debt at the same level as where it was when she started.

Her position in year 5 is now as follows:

➠ She owes $50,000 on her home and $150,000 on her investment, a total loan of $200,000 (as above).

➡ She pays $3,125 interest on her own home, and $9,375 on her investment loan, a total of $12,500 in loan interest (as above).

➡ She receives back $2,813 in tax (as her investment loan is still drawn at $150,000, fully tax deductible).

➡ She actually only pays out the equivalent of $9,687 in loan interest, making her $563 better off.

Of course, she would now pay this extra money straight into her home loan, improving her position even further. By being more careful about both the type of loan she chose and by managing the entire loan portfolio more effectively, Lesley has maximised her tax position and enhanced her ability to invest further.

Is This Allowed?

I have received several emails recently in which readers have told me of well-meaning accountants advising them that the tax department does not allow this method of loan repayment as there is a problem with the 'acquittal' of extra repayments into the personal debt. The next section in this chapter will show you how you can still take advantage of this tax minimisation strategy and keep well within tax law too.

> Interest-only loans are an important part of your investment strategy...

Interest-only loans are an important part of your investment strategy, particularly where you still have personal debt to repay. Using them wisely will result in a clear acceleration of your property acquisition.

Lines of Credit

Contrary to popular belief, a line of credit is not just a loan whereby you 'put in all of your money and use a credit card'! While 'mortgage reduction' organisations all around Australia today are still cashing in by introducing people to this method of using the bank's money, the lenders themselves are reportedly reviewing the wisdom of making available a continuous line of credit to people who cannot prove that they have the capacity to manage it effectively.

Let us first take a look at what a line of credit really is, and then move on to discussing some effective and responsible ways of using one for your investment portfolio.

What Is It?

A line of credit works like your credit card, except that it is 'secured' lending, as opposed to the non-secured lending you receive with a credit card.

It works like this: the bank gives you a 'credit limit' which is based on both the value of the security (property) which you are giving them, and your own personal borrowing capacity (see earlier section—Qualifying for a Loan). In most cases, a bank will allow you to borrow up to 80% of the market value of your home without lender's mortgage insurance, and up to 90% with lender's mortgage insurance.

A line of credit looks like an ordinary home loan (with interest rates generally the same or similar), except that you may move around within your predetermined limit in any way you like, providing you meet your commitments. This means that you must pay the interest bill when it falls due, and remain within the credit limit provided.

For example, you may have a limit of $100,000, provided to you against a property worth $125,000. During the month you can put money in and take money out as often as you want to—usually at the bank, through an ATM, or in a store using EFTPOS. The only rule is that, by the end of the month, your balance cannot be any higher than $100,000, and since the bank will add on interest (based on whatever your balance has been, each day), then you need to make sure that at least this interest is paid.

Note that with a line of credit there is not really a repayment—each time you put money in you are allowed to take it all back out again as long as you leave enough to meet the interest bill. So, where you have been putting more money in than you take out, you will actually reduce the balance. If you then have a month where you take out more than you put in it will not matter, you will have created enough 'equity' in the loan for this equity to pay the interest payment for you. (For more detailed information about using lines of credit, read the relevant sections in *How to Make Your Money Last as Long as You Do*.)

> A 'good' line of credit will be portable, so that you can move it from property to property.

A 'good' line of credit will be portable, so that you can move it from property to property. This can be a boon, and make moving and even upgrading so much easier. For example, consider Mark, who had a line of credit for $150,000 which he used to buy a house worth $200,000.

> After five years Mark had paid the loan down to $100,000 (but retained the limit of $150,000). Mark decided to move, and his house was now worth $230,000. He found a house he liked for $270,000.
>
> At present, he has $130,000 equity in the house—since he only 'owes' $100,000. If he sells his property for $230,000, technically he has $130,000 in cash. But, instead of having to discharge the loan and establish a new one, he can move the loan he already has. He 'draws back' the $50,000 equity which he has in the loan (making the loan balance $150,000 again), and uses the $230,000 he receives for his house, plus the $50,000 he drew back, which gives him enough for the new house (including costs to buy).

The bank simply swaps over the security, releasing the one they have and taking the new one. Mark's position has progressed like this:

⇨ He started with a debt of $150,000 on a house worth $200,000 ($50,000 equity).

⇨ After five years he had a debt of $100,000 on a house worth $230,000 ($130,000 equity).

↪ He swapped over the securities and drew back the equity in the loan, giving him a loan of $150,000 on a house worth $270,000 ($120,000 equity). The only reason for the difference in equity position ($10,000) is the purchasing costs.

In using his line of credit in this way, he has saved the costs and the hassles of establishing a new loan, and since he did not increase the limit available to him, he did not even need to make a new loan application.

The Drawbacks

Of course, the very features which make a line of credit one of the most flexible options around are often the catalysts for problems for many people. Given its accessibility, and the fact that you never have to pay this debt off, these types of loans are bad news for people with no self-discipline. In addition, the ease with which many lenders provide an 'increase' to limits as your home value increases results in many people being caught up in a loan which they simply keep extending, often past the level at which they can comfortably meet the commitments. If you are unable to manage a budget well enough to provide savings and investment funds for your future, then you are not advised to use a line of credit for any reason.

Lines of Credit for Investing

Having warned against lines of credit for some people, I am pleased to say that I, and many of my clients, find a line of credit a wonderful product of the '90s which will continue to provide huge benefits to investors well into the millennium. But be aware that not all lines of credit are equal—only a select few lenders offer lines of credit with features and benefits which make investing and the accounting involved a breeze. Here's what to look out for.

Split Facilities

A line of credit must have the ability to be split for dual purposes. Here is where the warnings from accountants about tax effectiveness can be simply addressed. A little bit of history may help you to better understand just what may be troubling your accountant.

In the 1980s, when investing in property began to catch on, investors would simply extend, or refinance, their home loans in order to access the funds needed to buy another property. For example, a home owner with a house worth $250,000 and a debt of $100,000 may have purchased another house for $150,000, increasing (or refinancing) the loan to $260,000 (original loan amount plus new property plus purchase costs).

Where the loan was a standard P&I loan (the most common), the accounting in this instance was fairly easy to undertake—in the example above the owner-occupied home represented around 38% of the total loan and the investment represented around 62%. At tax time, the accountant would claim 62% of the year's interest as a tax deduction.

When lines of credit first became popular, people began using them for investing, in the same manner as outlined in the previous pages—except that a complication arose.

You see, the aim of a line of credit is to put all of your funds in, and only draw out what is necessary to live on. In doing so you expect to make some inroads in to the principal, thereby paying down this loan more quickly (see mortgage reduction, Chapter 12).

As they had always done, accountants acquitted these loans in the same manner—regardless of what had been paid in or drawn out, the interest on the loan was claimed according the original proportions on the loan (the prior example showing a 62%/38% split).

The tax department took exception to this and decided that, where one loan was used for this dual purpose, all payments into the loan (personal income, tax refunds, rents) would be treated as a repayment of the principal as per the proportions worked out at the start. But, all drawings had to be considered as personal drawings, therefore attributed only to the personal portion of the debt.

The bottom line was that while this meant repayments were attributed to each part of the loan, drawings all came from the personal portion. The result was a personal portion which increased at an alarming rate, while the investment loan reduced equally alarmingly, and so did the tax effectiveness of investing in property.

And so was born the split loan—with the blessing of the tax department. Providing the facility is split at the commencement of the loan (that is, one loan divided into two or more accounts each with a designated purpose), then you may claim all of the interest being charged on the investment split as a tax deduction.

In fact, this can then be taken one step further, and true accelerated mortgage reduction can occur, providing the property in question provides a positive cash flow.

Lines of Credit and Accelerated Mortgage Reduction

You may remember that in Chapter 5 an example was given where the purchase of positive cash flow property accelerated the personal mortgage of Ted and Teresa. To achieve this in practice, a line of credit with a split facility is the most effective tool you can find. This way, you will be able to pay all funds (rents, tax refunds, personal income and any positive cash flow) into the first account (which should be your personal account), and pay the interest bill on the second account as and when it falls due. Visually, it would look something like Figure 9.1.

Figure 9.1

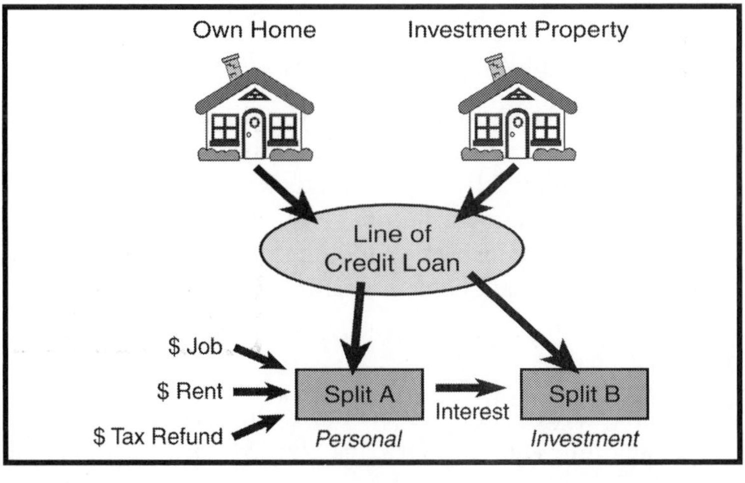

Note that:

- ↩ All funds are going into the personal portion of this loan, and are therefore *offsetting* the interest being accrued.

- ↩ If interest is being offset, less interest is being added to the loan so more of the principal is being paid off by each dollar which is left in the loan.

- ↩ Only the interest is being paid off the investment portion, leaving it fully drawn and maintaining maximum tax advantages.

- ↩ The *overall* balance of the loan is still decreasing and equity in the portfolio is being achieved—the reduction is seen in the personal portion, that is the non–tax-deductible portion.

- ↩ All expenses for the investment property must come from the personal portion as this is where the rent is being placed. If the expenses were met from the investment portion (assuming the limit on this portion had equity in it to allow this) then this would increase the original loan and this is when trouble may come from the tax department (see Chapter 10 for more on this).

A split loan can not only keep the tax department happy, it will allow you to reduce borrowing in the right area and obtain the maximum advantage from using mortgage reduction principles.

The Ability to Rearrange and/or Increase the Limits

When you set up a line of credit loan, you will be provided with a credit limit which you cannot exceed unless you apply for an increase. If the original loan amount was provided at the maximum loan-to-valuation ratio at the time (say, 90% for example), you would not be able to increase your limit unless the market value of the properties the bank holds as security increases.

A Personal Example

One of the things I like most about my line of credit is the fact that, at any time and for a very small fee ($10 at my bank at the time of writing), I can rearrange the limits on each of my sub-accounts (the various split accounts I have within the loan). For $100 I can add a sub-account as needed. This is very handy when investing. Here's an example of what I have done:

- ➪ When I first established the loan, it was just one account and represented only personal debt, as I had used the money to buy the house in which I lived. After 18 months, the combined effect of using a mortgage reduction strategy and the increase in value to my property meant that I had the deposit to buy an investment property.

- ➪ Using the methods outlined in earlier chapters, I bought an investment property and so had two properties held by the bank. My one loan was then split in two, and I continued to apply all funds to the personal portion as outlined in the previous example.

- ➪ As the personal portion decreased, I applied to rearrange the limits—that is, I kept the overall limit the same, but decreased the limit available on my personal portion while increasing the limit available on my investment portion. This then began to free-up that extra money so that I could get it ready for the next property acquisition, making my deposit available from funds marked as 'investment' rather than from those marked as 'personal'. This makes tax time easier as I am technically never using personal funds as a deposit.

- ➪ As soon as the combined effect of the decreasing balance (so an increasing 'available limit') and the rising market values of the properties I hold gives me enough money for the deposit on another property (that is 20% plus costs), I simply add the new security property and apply to increase the existing limit to pay for the property.

In applying to have the limits rearranged in this way, a new loan application is not required provided you are not seeking additional funds. Where I wish to add a new security and therefore increase the overall borrowings, I must apply all over again and be qualified for my 'new loan', although this new loan is really just an increase to my existing loan.

As a practical example for how this all really works, look at Chapter 11. There you will find many examples covering the different needs of different investors.

Ability to Add and Release Securities

The final advantage of having a line of credit is its ability to have properties added and taken away with ease. Under normal circumstances, when you sell a property you must have the mortgage discharged. In the case where you have a 'melting pot' of securities (that is one loan and several properties), this usually means that you must establish a new loan on the remaining properties, and this can be costly.

A good line of credit will have the feature of being able to do what is known as a 'partial release of security' and a 'substitution of security'. The former task is where one of the properties is released, and the limit of the loan adjusted to have a final loan-to-valuation ratio of no more than 80% (or 90% as the case may be). The latter task is where one security is taken away and another added. In this case the limit will either be left as is (providing the total value of securities held allows the required loan-to-valuation ratio) or increased or decreased accordingly.

Note that it will only be in the case where the limit needs to be *increased* that a new application will be required—in other cases you will not have to go through the application process again, and you will only need to pay a nominal fee for the task to be completed (in addition to valuation fees where they have been required). This can be very handy for some people as the following example shows.

> John owned four investment properties when he was made redundant from his job and chose to take early retirement. About a year later, John wanted to sell one of his properties and buy another. Unfortunately, because John did not have a job any more, he would usually not be able to apply for a loan to buy the new property. However, he had the right loan, and because the values of the two properties were quite similar (and John had some equity available in his

loan), he was able to simply apply for a 'substitution of security' —in doing so no loan application was required.

Since this method of security substitution is rather rare, John's solicitor was unsure of how to approach this; however, familiar as I am with the process, I was able to lead him (and many other solicitors doing the same job) through the process so that all things went smoothly.

Are All Lines of Credit Like This?

It is important to know that very few lines of credit actually come with these kinds of features, and even more important to know that few brokers or 'property investment experts' have a clue as to just how advantageous the right loan can truly be. Many lenders offer lines of credit which simply do not stack up. Be sure you ask about all of the features and be sure that, at the very least, your proposed line of credit has all of the features outlined in this chapter.

Lines of credit may have slightly higher interest rates in some cases, however when you consider the wide range of other features and benefits, then a true line of credit is the only loan which can provide the flexibility you need when building your property portfolio. Used correctly, even a higher interest rate can result in less interest paid overall. The right line of credit will remain right for the entire term of your portfolio, saving you time, effort and, most importantly, money!

> Used correctly, even a higher interest rate can result in less interest paid overall.

Applying for the Loan

When you make any application for a loan, you must present an honest account of your personal financial circumstances. Beware of loan brokers who suggest withholding information from a loan application. I have come across cases of brokers who assist their clients to omit information and to falsify documents. This is serious and is called 'mortgage fraud', carrying with it penalties which can include jail terms. Although the finance broker industry is largely unregulated, all players still have to follow the law and are also covered by the Trade Practices Act.

Each lender will have their own application process. While some may want your entire life story, others will have a fairly simple two-page document. Either way, once your personal details have been provided, there are two common sections in all applications.

Declaration

The declaration is the part you sign declaring that all information you have provided is true and correct at the time of application. By signing this, you are guaranteeing the bank that you are telling them the truth and providing all information to the best of your knowledge.

CAL Permission

This section requires you to give the lender permission to run a credit check with Credit Advantage Limited. Formerly known as CRAA (Credit Reporting Agency Australia), this organisation provides to lenders a report with detailed information about your credit history. Credit Advantage holds a database of information on almost anyone who has ever applied for credit in the past (whether or not that credit was 'taken up'), applied for a residential tenancy, or been in arrears or defaulted on a loan without an arrangement with the lender.

Almost every one has a credit report, and few people realise the extent of the information in one of these reports. Where you have had some difficulty with a repayment, and you have been unable to reach a satisfactory arrangement with the lender, you may well have an entry on your report about this difficulty. If you have ever been bankrupt, this will also be noted.

Having an entry on this report does not automatically preclude you from having a loan approved. If you know that you may have an entry, it is far better to declare it to the lender before they find out, as if you can provide a plausible explanation the lender may still approve your application.

A CAL report can sometimes be inaccurate or out of date. For example, you may have had an entry for non-payment of a debt which you have subsequently paid, but since notation of the payment has not been made, it will appear that you still owe this money. If you are refused credit due to a CAL entry of which you are unaware, or which you know has been remedied, you can apply to see your CAL report by phoning them, or by visiting their website. If the information is in fact incorrect, contact the agency and they will rectify this for you.

Required Documentation

Your application for finance must be accompanied by the following documentation:

↝ Current proof of income.

↝ Proof of expected rental return.

↝ Evidence of rent currently being received.

↝ Proof of good conduct on any current loans (letter from current bank or loan statements).

↝ Rates notices on any properties being given as security.

↝ Social security notices if you receive benefits.

↝ 100 points of identification, such as a birth certificate or passport, along with a driver's licence or other photo identification.

Lenders may have additional requirements, depending on your own personal circumstances. Most lenders can provide you with a written list of what they will require.

It usually will only take two to four days for a loan to be approved. Once conditional approval is received, the bank will arrange for a valuation to be carried out to be sure that the security is worth what you say it is. Where the loan-to-valuation ratio is low (under 75%) some banks will accept the purchase price without the need for a valuation to be done. Do not exchange or otherwise sign a binding contract for any property purchase until the bank has provided you with a written letter of approval.

Lenders can be positively pedantic when it comes to the approval process. If you are prepared before you apply you can save a lot of time by providing everything the bank needs up front.

Non-Traditional Sources of Finance

A few years ago I went to the USA with the family. I remember our first trip to Walmart. We were astounded at the selection offered for each type of food. There was an entire aisle just for popcorn (I can't even find the popcorn in my supermarket!).

Things are getting a little like this when it comes to lending in Australia. Not only are there dozens of lenders to choose from, each of them has a veritable stable of loans.

Today non-bank lenders are more popular than ever before. They offer low-interest-rate finance and no-frills loans. Be careful though— loans from these sources can take forever to settle and very often come with unclear conditions which make early pay-out very expensive, often outweighing the benefits of the lower rate. If you do decide to refinance a non-bank loan, sometimes they can take much longer than usual to settle, since there is usually an underwriter providing the funds who must approve the discharge.

Solicitor and finance broker funds are another source of finance —ones which have certainly made the news in recent times. While some of these may be legitimate sources of money, many are badly managed and the investors who provide the funds in the first place are finding they have lost their precious savings. This is usually attributed to lack of due diligence in the approval of loans, and unreasonable valuations which have allowed more money to be advanced to a borrower than the security property is actually worth. Solicitors' funds can also be very expensive, and usually have a fairly short term, at the end of which they must be refinanced into another loan.

Lastly, the past few years have given birth to lenders providing money to 'credit impaired' borrowers, or people with unstable employment history or with businesses without financial statements. Money such as this usually comes at a premium, both in interest rates and establishment fees.

If you need to use a non-traditional source of finance in order to invest (with the exception of the larger non-bank lenders), I would suggest that you may not be ready to invest at all. In addition, your investment will need to perform much more profitably just to cover the extra costs of this kind of finance.

In Summary

The most effective loan for your property investment will have the following features:

- ➥ The option of interest only, so that personal debt can receive the benefits of your cash flow first, after which you will begin to also pay principal on your investment loan.

- ➥ The ability to park income in the loan to offset interest— even investment loans need to be repaid eventually, so you will want to use 'mortgage reduction' principles once your personal debt is finalised.

- ➥ A reasonable variable rate, with an option to fix if you really need to.

- ➥ The ability to split one loan into several sub-accounts for easier accounting of investment loans.

- ➥ The ability to alter the respective limits on each sub-account that you have in the loan portfolio.

- ➥ The ability to increase your limit without needing to refinance.

- ➥ The option to add or substitute (or release) a security without having to rewrite the loan.

- ➥ The ability to add extra accounts as you need them.

- ➥ The option to redraw to the full original approved amount of the loan—lines of credit requiring a regular, principal repayment are not true lines of credit.

- ➥ Access through ATMs and EFTPOS so that this loan can become the one and only account you will ever need, eliminating expensive bank fees on unnecessary accounts.

Shop around and be sure you know exactly what you are looking for. Accepting anything less than the above may seem like a minor adjustment now but later on you may well wish that you had been more discerning in your choice.

Conclusion

If I have included something in this book, then it is because that subject is of vital importance to you. My experience with investors is that obtaining the loan to buy an investment is one of the least-investigated areas.

Make no mistake, the success of your entire portfolio can be either enhanced by the careful selection of the right loan product or hampered by the wrong selection. If you already have property investments, then you must look over your loan structure and, if necessary, make the changes now before you waste any more money. While there may be a short-term cost for you, the long-term savings will most definitely make this cost one well worth incurring.

Tax and Positive Cash Flow Property

➠ **It is worthwhile considering using an accountant once you begin to invest.**

➠ **You must know what you can and cannot claim from the tax department.**

➠ **You should claim your tax back regularly, not once a year.**

➠ **It is important to keep up with tax laws because they change often.**

I WISH I HAD A DOLLAR for every person who has ever asked me if I know a good accountant (by the time I am finished this book, I won't have a single professional friend left!). It's not that there are no good accountants—there are many. It's just that they have expertise in particular areas, which means that if you are going to consult an accountant about your property investments, your salary package and your business income, then you may need up to three different accountants!

For those who are basic salary and wage earners, you may, in the past, have completed the 'tax pack' on your own. If this is you, it is worthwhile considering using an accountant once you begin to invest. There will be a cost involved but this cost should more than pay for itself with the savings you may make on items you might not have known you could claim.

Whether you intend to use an accountant or would like to attempt to complete your own tax return, it is vital that you understand just what you can and cannot claim from the tax department. This way, you can be sure of getting all of the benefit from your investing that you possibly can.

The Point

If you think that there have been a lot of changes to bank interest rates over the past two years, you should see how many times tax law has changed! In addition to the law itself changing, cases arise every day which test the boundaries of any law and, where a particular rule is subject to interpretation, the tax department makes decisions which then become a precedent for future cases.

If you are going to become an investor (or if you are already one) then it is paramount that you become educated about investing. This does not mean you have to do everything for yourself—but it does mean you must have the right amount of knowledge to be sure that others are doing the right thing for you. This chapter covers a good deal of information about taxation and property, and should give you the basis for further research of your own.

Income Tax

Imagine living in a country where there was no income tax! So many of the wonderful things which we take for granted simply would not be there. Health and aged care would suffer, as would our parklands, roads, etc. Some people believe our income tax system to be unfair, and from the perspective of those in the higher tax brackets this may well seem true. The issue here is that, as yet, a viable alternative has not been offered, and even when the system is changed (such as with the introduction of the GST) half of the country disagrees!

Income tax is a fact of life for all income earners in this country. While tax evasion (arrangements to avoid tax which are outside the law) is illegal and punishable by a fine or even a jail term, tax avoidance (arrangements to avoid tax which are within the law) is every taxpayer's right!

> Income tax is a fact of life for all income earners in this country.

With the introduction of the GST in July 2000, our income tax system underwent a change, with tax cuts for most people the result.

The tax rates for 2005–06 are as follows:

$0–$6,000	*Nil*
$6,001–$21,600	*15¢ for each $1 over $6,000*
$21,601–$63,000	*$2,340 plus 30¢ for each $1 over $21,600*
$63,001–$95,000	*$14,760 plus 42¢ for each $1 over $63,000*
Over $95,000	*$28,200 plus 47¢ for each $1 over $95,000*

(See the tax calculator in Destiny Finsoft to quickly calculate your tax.)

A person earning $65,000 would pay tax as follows:

On the first $6,000	*Nil*
On the next $15,600	*15% or $2,340*
On the next $41,400	*30% or $12,420*
On the next 2,000	*42% or $840*

The total tax bill for this person would be $15,600.

In addition, there will be a Medicare levy, perhaps an additional Medicare levy for high-income earners or a rebate for low-income earners, and a host of other rebates and allowances depending on your personal circumstances.

Pay as you go (PAYG) income earners have very little access to any kind of tax relief, as there is little that the average person can claim if employed by someone else. Depending on your occupation, you may have claims such as laundry, travel or study costs, but this is generally not the case.

Once you acquire your first investment, however, the situation changes remarkably, and you have many things for which you can make a claim. Why is this? Quite simply, the government encourages us to invest within our own country through a range of tax benefits. Not only can this help to prevent our money from going offshore, it can address housing needs for those people who must rent, a problem which would be left to the government if private landlords did not own property.

Stephen called me last year and said (quite proudly, I might add), "I have paid too much tax this year!" "OK," I replied, "Congratulations!" "Well," he said, "I am going to buy this great property which I saw because then I will cut my tax."

This sounded good in theory. But let's see what Stephen was proposing.

> The property would cost $150,000. The return would be $150 a week. Stephen was in the 30% tax bracket, earning $58,000.
>
> The property costs would be $10,000 in interest, and another $3,500 in costs each year.

Let's look at Stephen's position before and after the purchase.

Before he made the purchase:

Income	$58,000
Tax	$13,260
Net pay	**$44,740**

After he made the purchase:

Income	$58,000
Rent (assuming full occupancy)	$7,800
Total gross income	$65,800
Claimable expenses	$13,500

Taxable income	$52,300
Tax	**$11,550**

Yes, Stephen *has* reduced his tax payable. But what does this look like as far as cash in hand goes?

Total income	$65,800
less	
Expenses	$13,500
less	
Tax	$11,550
Net pay	**$40,750**

The pleasure of giving the tax department $1,710 less tax has resulted in Stephen losing $3,990 from his net pay each year! I know what you are saying—but what about the fact that he is buying an appreciating asset? What about... What if...

Yes, that is exactly the problem—'what ifs'! And, because we do not know 'what if', this would appear to me to be a big gamble on Stephen's part—spending $3,990 on the chance that he may make some money.

Since you have already had this lecture in previous chapters, I will move on quickly. You know that investing carries tax deductions, and despite the fact that this should not be the *reason* why you would invest, it can certainly be a benefit. Chosen wisely, this benefit can mean money in your pocket. So, let us look at just what we can and cannot claim from the tax department.

Investing and Tax

Depending on the investment, the government allows you to offset the costs of having an investment against income earned from that investment as well as other sources. In addition to the obvious costs of holding the investment, you may claim some items which are considered 'on paper' only—that is you do not actually pay for them, but you claim them as if you had. This of course means that you get the tax back, but you have not paid out anything first. Isn't it great when you hear about something that is actually in your favour?

Let us have a look at the things which the tax department will allow you to claim once you have acquired an investment property.

Capital Costs

Capital costs are the purchasing costs which you incurred when you bought the property. In addition, a capital cost includes any money spent on capital improvements (such as extensions, pergolas, driveways, etc.) and also money which you may spend when you dispose of the property. Careful distinction must be made between the replacement of an item of plant (such as replacing the hot water service) and an improvement (such as rendering the brickwork).

You cannot claim capital costs as a tax deduction against earned income. You can, however, offset them against capital gain made at the point of sale, effectively reducing the gain and so the capital gains tax which must be paid. This is done by adding the cost of these items to the purchase price of the property—making the 'cost base' of the property higher. An example of this will be given in the capital gains tax section later in this chapter.

Revenue Costs

Revenue costs are all of those costs which are incurred in the process of earning the rental income. Expenses which may be able to be claimed include:

⇝ Advertising for a tenant.

⇝ Loan interest and bank fees.

⇝ Borrowing costs, over a five-year period or the time the investment is held, whichever is shorter. This includes establishment fees, loan stamp duty, solicitor's costs, lender's mortgage insurance and valuation fees.

- Body corporate fees, rates, energy and water bills.

- Land tax.

- Cleaning, mowing, gardening, repairs and maintenance.

- Building, contents, liability and landlord's insurance.

- Accountancy fees, property management fees, legal fees (not relating to the actual purchase), tax related expenses.

- Lease costs.

- Pest control.

- Quantity surveyor's fees.

- Security patrol fees.

- Stationery, postage and telephone.

- Travel expenses when inspecting the property.

The list goes on, and your accountant will be able to tell you what is included as a viable property expense. You cannot claim:

- Stamp duty on conveyancing.

- Expenses on the property not actually paid by you, such as water and electricity paid by the tenant.

- Expenses that do not relate to the renting of the property, such as your expenses on a holiday house which is leased for only part of a year.

In some cases, expenses must be apportioned between deductible and non-deductible. For example, where:

- The property is only let part of the year and you use it the other part.

- Only part of the property is income-producing (such as a room or flat).

- You combine a holiday with inspecting your property, you must only claim a portion of the travel costs. Beware the salesperson who uses the 'tax deductible' holiday angle as a way to get you to buy a property—it may not work out this way.

Note that with all of the above expenses, the cost is incurred before you can claim it as a deduction. This means that, at the very most, for each one dollar you pay out, you can only receive 47¢ back (or a 47¢ tax deduction). This is, of course, provided this is the tax bracket in which you earn your income. For the majority of people who pay tax at only 30%, 30¢ is the most they can get back, while a low-income earner will receive 17¢, or even nothing (since you cannot get back tax you have not paid!).

You must still pay the other 53¢ (or 70¢ or 83¢) yourself from the rent received or, where this is not enough (as in negative gearing), from your own pocket.

Depreciation

There have been many changes in the way that depreciation can be claimed as a tax deduction, with the most recent changes applying from 2004. This section will deal with any properties purchased after 21 September 2004. For information about depreciation on properties acquired before that date, speak with your accountant or contact the Australian Tax Office.

> There have been many changes in the way that depreciation can be claimed as a tax deduction...

Depreciation can be divided into two sections—depreciation on plant and equipment (furniture, fixtures and fittings) and depreciation on the building (capital works deductions).

Depreciation on Furniture, Fixtures or Fittings

Where an item of furniture, or a fixture or fitting not a part of the building, is used to produce an income, then the cost of its depreciation may be claimed against earned income. I recall having a rather heated discussion with a gentleman over the claiming of these items once. He stated that the only reason the tax department lets you claim depreciation was because you eventually had to pay for replacement of these items anyway! He is right—you do have to pay to replace these items, but you have to replace them whether you intend to claim the depreciation or not. So, you may as well claim the tax deductions, so that you can produce the positive cash flow which you can then save up to replace these items.

The rate at which you can depreciate an item will depend on its effective life, and is anywhere between one and twenty years. The commissioner of taxation has determined the average effective life on a long list of common items, however the taxpayer may make his or her own estimate of effective life, if it can be substantiated with evidence.

For example, the commissioner has declared that carpets have an effective life of ten years. This would mean that I could depreciate the cost of the carpet in my rental properties over a ten-year period. However, the carpet in my holiday house takes a lot of wear and tear. There is a continuous stream of holiday-makers, all of whom traipse the sand from the beach straight in the door. And, since the house sleeps ten people, there is much heavier traffic than usual. I would certainly have a case for claiming that the effective life of the carpet in my holiday house is in fact five years, not ten.

How is Depreciation Calculated?

There are two ways in which you can claim the depreciation—the prime cost method or the diminishing value method. As each of these methods requires quite a complicated formula to calculate, it is far better for you to ask your accountant which method would be most advantageous to your personal circumstances. The Australian Tax Office website allows you to download some great information on these—they also have available a guide to depreciation, which includes worksheets for calculating depreciation.

The list of items you can claim is too extensive to reproduce here. As a rule of thumb, if the item can be moved, then it is an item of plant and can be claimed as plant and equipment (fixtures, fittings and furniture) depreciation. If, on the other hand, it is part of the setting for a rent-producing activity, rather than a fixture, fitting or piece of furniture, then it would be claimed as a part of the capital works deductions. Different rules apply to capital works deductions.

These items may include things such as:

↪ In-ground swimming pools, saunas and spas.

↪ Plumbing and gas fittings.

↪ Garage doors, roller shutters and skylights.

↪ Sinks, tubs, baths, washbowls and toilets.

The distinction should be that if you cannot move it, then it is part of the scenery and qualifies for capital works deductions.

Capital Works Deductions

Capital works deductions are allowable deductions where you may claim the costs of construction of a building over a set period of time. The amount you can claim is limited (of course!) to 100% of the cost of the construction.

You see, although property appreciates in value, in fact it is the land only which is appreciating. The house or building itself depreciates as it gets older. When you buy a property, the tax department accepts that the building portion of this property will depreciate and become worth less, and so they allow you to claim a tax deduction based on this premise.

To know just how much you can claim, you must know when the building was first constructed. The following rules apply:

↪ Where the construction began before 18 July 1985, you are not able to claim anything.

↪ Where the construction occurred between 18 July 1985 and 15 September 1987 and the property is residentially leased, you are able to claim 4% of the construction costs, for a period of 25 years.

↪ Where the construction occurred after 15 September 1987 and the property is residentially leased, you are able to claim 2.5% for 40 years.

↪ Where the property is short-term let (that is a tourism property), the 4% applies.

Any structural improvements which were carried out after 26 February 1992 may also be depreciated at the above rates.

So, if you purchased a residential property for $150,000 in 1999 which had been constructed in 1994, you could claim capital works deductions for another 35 years. If this property had a construction cost of, say, $90,000, then you would be able to write-off $2,250 against your tax every year, without actually spending this money. If you are earning income in the top marginal rate of tax, this would mean that you would receive $1,058 of your tax back.

Now, add this to possible depreciation on furniture, fixtures and fittings, and you may have quite a healthy sum of tax to get back. This tax refund, when added to the rent you are receiving, may be enough to more than cover your expenses and bank interest, and this is how we achieve positive cash flow property!

New Effective Life

What if you do not know what the construction costs were? Unless you buy a new property, it is highly unlikely that the current owner will even know what was spent on the building.

This is OK! All you need to do is retain the services of a 'quantity surveyor'. The job of the surveyor is to provide for you what is known as a 'depreciation schedule'. This schedule will not only make an estimate of what the construction costs would have been, but it provides for you a list of all of the furniture, fixtures and fittings, and gives each of them a value at the time of your purchase.

While you are only allowed to claim the remaining years of capital works deductions (so, in the example above, only 35 years remained), all other depreciable items are given what is known as a 'new effective life'. This means that a value is put on each item at the time you purchase the property, and you may then claim the depreciation over this new effective life.

I will point out here that it can be a little harder to estimate the effective life of what is essentially a second-hand item, and the recommendations provided by the commissioner will probably not be appropriate, as they will assume that items are new. You can, however, ask the quantity surveyor to make recommendations about the effective life of the items on which he or she is providing a value.

A quantity surveyor will charge you a fee (usually around $400), but this fee is well worthwhile. Where a property is new, you may like to make it a condition of sale that the vendor or developer provides a depreciation schedule upon settlement. Be careful how you word this condition, though. We recently included just such a condition in the contracts for a client buying a property from our Destiny Positive Cash Flow Property Register. We asked for a depreciation schedule, but received a hand-written list which included ten items of furniture and the original price of each! Somehow I don't think the tax department will be happy with this.

Don't I Have to Pay Back Capital Works Deductions?

This is a very confusing area, one which few people truly understand. In essence, if you are claiming that the building on your property has depreciated, then at the point of sale the amount of capital works deductions you have claimed should be deducted from the price you originally paid for the property, for assessing capital gains tax. People who prefer other investment vehicles to property will often use this as an argument against property, saying that capital works deductions are not really the benefit that they appear to be because you pay at the end anyway. However, even with this being the case, the benefits still fall to you.

> Kylie bought a property in 1990 valued at $150,000, which had been constructed in 1988 for $90,000. She then sold the property in 2000 for $250,000. Her cost base for the property (once she added purchasing costs) was $160,000 and the realised price (once she deducted selling costs) was $240,000. She did not claim any capital works deductions because she did not want to have to pay extra capital gains tax at the time of disposal.

The gain of $80,000 would be taxable at half the rate of gain (see capital gains tax section of this chapter), or $40,000. At the 47% tax rate, this would mean a tax bill of $18,800, making Kylie's net gain from this property $61,200.

> Lyn bought a similar property during the same time period. However, she claimed capital works deductions on the building, at the rate of $2,250 a year. This gave her $1,058 a year back in tax.

At the time of sale, the entire amount claimed as capital works deductions must be subtracted from the cost base. In reality Lyn's position would be:

Cost base	**$137,500**
($150,000 + $10,000 purchasing costs less $22,500 claimed as capital works deductions)	
Realised price	$240,000
On paper gain	$102,500
Taxable gain	$51,250
Tax to be paid	$24,087
Real gross gain	$80,000 (as for Kylie)
Net gain after tax	**$55,913**

Note that the difference between Kylie and Lyn was that Lyn paid $5,287 more in capital gains tax, yet she received, over the time, a total of $10,575 of tax benefits (her tax breaks on the capital works deductions). Given the time value of money, and the fact that the positive cash flow was helping Lyn to acquire more property and a greater exposure to capital gain over time, then the true value of this tax benefit would in fact be far greater.

Better still, there is one sure way never to have to 'pay back' this capital works deductions benefit—don't sell your property! Since your aim is to create an income for life, then you will want to keep the property forever and enjoy the income stream it provides, without ever having to worry about capital gains tax at all.

Interest on the Loan

As listed earlier, interest on the loan you use to buy the property is a tax deduction. However, there is always some confusion over exactly what can be claimed.

If you have a principal and interest loan, you cannot claim the *repayments* of the loan, you may only claim the interest portion of that repayment. This is because the principal repayment portion of each instalment you make to your loan is actually buying you equity, or a bit more ownership of the property. Since you are claiming the depreciation on that equity, you cannot also claim that part of the repayment (and you couldn't even if you were not claiming depreciation).

This is OK because, remember, that for each extra one dollar of equity you own, that is one dollar more exposure you personally have to that rising market, and one dollar more toward buying the next property.

Purpose

Tax deductibility on an investment debt is all about purpose. You may only claim interest on a debt if the purpose for getting that debt was to buy an income-producing investment.

If you borrow to buy an investment property, but add $20,000 to the debt to also buy a car for your own personal use, you can only claim the interest on the portion of the debt used for the property, even if you only have one loan for both.

If you own a home which you subsequently move from, and you begin to rent this home out, you may claim the interest on any remaining debt. If, however, you used that home to raise a debt to buy or build a new home for yourself, then you can only claim the interest on that part of the debt which was attributable to the property producing the income. If the house you moved from had no debt, but you raised one against the house to enable you to buy another home, then none of the debt is tax deductible, as the purpose for the debt was for personal use.

Where you add to an investment debt to carry out improvements to your income-producing property, you may then claim the interest on the increased debt, as the purpose of the entire debt still remains 'to invest'.

These are just some of the reasons why a split loan is so important —it leaves no doubt as to the purpose of each debt, and it makes accounting a whole lot easier.

Travel Costs

You may claim the costs of travelling to an investment property to inspect the premises up to twice yearly, if the sole purpose for your trip is to inspect the premises. If you must fly to do so, you can claim the airfare and any accommodation, as long as you are doing nothing else but inspecting the property.

Where you combine a holiday with inspecting a property, then the tax department will not allow you to claim any airfares. You would be allowed to claim the cost of one night's accommodation plus any taxi or car fares only.

If you were to travel to inspect a property and you stayed, say, seven nights, the only way that you could legitimately claim all costs associated with this trip would be if you could prove that you spent the entire seven days on business which related to your investment. For example, you may have been carrying out repairs and maintenance, painting the property or otherwise attending to problems with the property. Once again the tax department is very strict about 'purpose' and the onus of proof is on you, the investor.

Capital Gains Tax

When you own an investment which makes a profit for you, and you subsequently dispose of that investment, you must pay capital gains tax on the gain. Since the changes to capital gains tax, the amount you are required to pay depends on both your own marginal rate of tax and on when you purchased the property.

The method for calculating capital gains tax on any property which was purchased before 21 September 1999 is as follows:

1. To the purchase price add on all capital costs (purchasing costs).

2. Add on any costs for improvement during that time.

3. Index the purchase price by using the relative CPI rate provided by the ATO. Note that any improvements must be indexed from the time the money was spent, not from when the property was purchased.

4. From the realised price take the sale costs.

5. The difference between the indexed purchase price and the adjusted realised price is the gain. This is added to your income for that year and you are taxed accordingly.

Where the property was purchased after 21 September 1999, then the method is simpler:

1. To the purchase price add any capital costs.

2. Add any costs to improve.

3. From the sale price take off sale costs

The difference is the gross gain. Take half of this gain and add it to your income for that year.

If you purchased your property before 21 September 1999, you may choose which method to use, but if your purchase was after this date, you must use the new method. It will depend on the amount of your gain and your marginal rate of tax as to which method will work out most profitable for you.

Where a property is rented for only part of the time which you own it, you may have a capital gains tax liability for those years in which you were claiming tax deductions. The above methods would be used to calculate the liability, with the purchase price being the value of the property as at the time it began to produce an income, and the sale price being the value at the time it stopped producing an income. Note that while the liability will be calculated for these periods, it will only become payable in the year of disposal. The same rules would apply where *part* of a property was let—at the time of disposal an assessment would need to be made of the contribution to capital gain that the portion of the property in question made.

You can minimise the amount of capital gains tax you must pay by being sure that you dispose of the property in a year when you are in a lower tax bracket (for example, the first year of retirement), and of course eliminate it altogether by never selling the property. You must realise, however, that the person to whom you 'will' your property (in the event of your death) will also inherit any capital gains tax liability you may have had.

Capital Loss

Where a property you dispose of incurs a capital loss (you get *less* than you paid for it), then you may carry forward this loss to write-off against any future capital gains you may make, from property or other investments. Sadly the reverse does not apply—you cannot carry forward a capital gain to write-off against future capital losses.

The new capital gains tax rules (where purchase price is no longer indexed) make it far less likely that your property will be worth less when you sell, unless of course you paid far too much for it in the first place!

Land Tax

Most property investors are unaware that they may at some time incur a land tax. This should not be a reason *not* to invest in property, however. Land tax is not too hefty and in fact is in itself tax deductible.

Land tax is a yearly tax which is levied in each state of Australia. Since it is a state regime, land tax is levied differently depending on where you own property. However, the advantage of this is that land tax is only levied if your land holdings in that state exceed the limits applied. This is as good an incentive as any for spreading your investments around the country.

When land tax is calculated, the land content only of any property you own is taken into consideration. The property in which you live is either exempt completely, or exempt providing it is within a certain threshold.

If you own a property jointly with another person, only the value of your portion of ownership is considered. If you own a strata titled property, only the small proportion of the actual land attached to your property (or attributed to the percentage of your ownership) is taxable. This makes a good case for considering strata titled property if you are concerned about paying land tax.

Land tax is indexed to inflation every year, with the tax-free threshold adjusted accordingly. Each state has a website which you can visit to find out more about land tax requirements.

Getting the Tax Back, Now!

Some people like to wait until the end of the year, and then claim their deductions in one lump sum. This is madness—the tax department will not pay you any interest on the tax it owes you, yet if you have it in your hand you can put it into your line of credit where you will save interest every day. I have a client whose accountant refuses to help her complete the necessary forms to get her tax back more regularly. He claims it is too 'messy' and easier to do at the end of the year. I told her that she needs a new accountant!

> Most property investors are unaware that they may at some time incur a land tax.

You are entitled to have the tax refund in your hand at the frequency with which you are paid your wages. In fact, you are not receiving the tax back at all—you are simply paying less tax in the first place.

When you earn your income, your payroll officer will deduct tax from your pay at the rate listed in the tax tables provided by the tax department. It is illegal to adjust this amount unless permission is given by the tax department.

To receive this permission, you must submit a 'Request to Vary Taxation' (section 15/15 form). This form used to be known, and is still often referred to, as a 221d certificate.

When you submit this request, you do not need to provide actual evidence—but you are warned that if your estimations of your new income (which should be an on-paper loss if you have purchased positive cash flow property) are too low, you may be penalised.

This form is very easy to complete. It requires you to estimate the rent for the year, the interest that you will pay on your loan, the costs you will incur and any depreciation or capital works deductions. You will also need to know what your other income for the year will be. I always make sure that I under-estimate the expenses and over-estimate the income, just by a small amount. This way, if I am wrong there is less likelihood that it will be by too much.

The trickiest part of applying for a variation to tax is the estimation of the depreciation. This is where you will find a proper depreciation schedule a vital tool and well worth the money it costs to obtain. You also need to be sure that your estimations are based on the number of months (or pay periods) remaining in the financial year.

Once you have submitted this form it will take around six weeks for your payroll officer to be advised of the change in tax rate for you. A new form must then be submitted each new financial year.

Conclusion

If you already own property, it is highly likely that there are things which you could have been claiming, yet didn't know about. It is possible to put in a retrospective claim, however you can only go back three years.

Knowing about and claiming those deductions to which you have a right is the most important part of obtaining a positive cash flow property. It forms the basis of your ability to buy property more quickly, and so contribute toward an income which will truly last for your lifetime, and beyond.

11 | Structuring for Positive Cash Flow Property

➠ **There are many ways in which a property purchase can be structured.**

➠ **If buying with your partner, in order to decide who should buy the property, work out where your cash flow is coming from.**

➠ **Restructuring your finances could save you money in fees.**

➠ **Remember that your personal circumstances can change rapidly.**

NOT LONG AFTER I SPOKE at an expo, a reader contacted one of my branches for some advice about her property portfolio. Her latest acquisition had been a lovely apartment in a sunny tourist spot, just the kind of destination many of us dream of for a holiday.

Since the client in question did not earn an income, yet her husband did, the salesperson suggested that she set up the property with a 99% ownership for her husband and a 1% ownership for her. The reasons for this structure were to give her husband all of the tax savings (since she had no tax to save), and to allow her to have a holiday up to twice a year to this marvellous destination, claiming the costs of that holiday as a tax deduction.

While this may be a wonderful selling point, sadly the tax department would not agree with this arrangement, for many reasons which will become apparent as you read on. I never cease to wonder at the fertile minds which think up these creative ideas! Sadly for the hapless purchasers, the salesperson is not the person responsible to the tax department for making an invalid claim, and by the time you put in your tax return, he or she will be long gone.

There are many ways in which a property purchase can be structured, but there must be a legitimate reason for choosing the structure you do. Buying a property for a tax-deductible trip should never be a prime motivator, and there are many legitimate reasons to think carefully about the way you will structure your purchase.

The Point

This chapter aims to outline some of the ways you can buy a property, and how you should structure your borrowings. By no means will any of the information here be actual legal advice, and investors are well-advised to seek independent legal advice before undertaking any structural arrangements.

Buying as a Sole Tenant (Owner)

Where a property is owned solely by one person, the income flows to that one person, and so do the taxation benefits. If this person takes a trip to inspect the property, and happens to take a spouse or companion, only those costs relating to the owner's trip (and only those relating to the property) can be claimed.

When the property is sold, all capital gains tax liabilities fall to the sole owner. A person buying a property in his or her own name cannot subsequently 'income split' with a spouse, or any other person. This can only occur where some other structure, like a trust or business structure, buys the property. Under these circumstances, other taxation treatment may also change.

Why Would I be a Sole Owner?

You would buy a property in one name only where one party earns a substantially higher income than the other, and the property uses negative gearing principles to provide a positive cash flow— that is the cash flow comes from an on-paper loss. Where the cash flow is a result of positive gearing instead, and tax deductions do not eliminate the profits, then you will want the property to be owned by the person with the lowest income.

This is because positive cash flow property comes as a result of tax back, and you want to get as much tax back as you can, so you will buy the investment in the name of the person who pays the most tax. Positive gearing, however, results in tax to be paid, so you would want the person paying tax at the lowest rate to own the investment (see page 188 for an example of how this works).

While the benefits are that all of the income, and therefore all of the tax benefits, flow to just one party, the drawback can be that the party without ownership may feel vulnerable in the case of a separation and divorce. In most states, family law determines that all assets of married (or de-facto) people are jointly owned for the purposes of a property settlement, overriding any legal ownership.

It is also vital that you are sure that your financial circumstances are not going to change—will the higher income earner remain so for the term of the investment, or is it just a short-term situation? If it is a short-term situation, joint ownership may be better for the long term even if there are benefit costs in the short term.

Borrowing as a Sole Owner

When you borrow as a sole owner, you will need to prove that you can satisfy income criteria on your own. If you need a spouse's income to help you to qualify, but do not want the spouse to be a joint owner, then some lenders will allow the spouse to become a 'guarantor' for borrowing purposes. Generally this will only be allowed where there is a personal relationship between the parties and a clear benefit to the guarantor can be demonstrated.

While the word guarantor strikes fear into the hearts of many people, don't worry. The responsibilities of a guarantor carry little difference to those of a borrower. If you are truly worried that your spouse may run off to Rio with another person, then I have to say you have more important things to consider than whether to become a guarantor or not!

> ...positive cash flow property comes as a result of tax back...

Buying as Joint Tenants

Usually, when we buy a house with a spouse we will do so as joint tenants. The distinction between a joint tenant and a tenant in common (see opposite) is made most clearly in death—where you are a joint tenant your share of the property falls *outside* your estate, automatically reverting to the other joint tenant(s) upon your death. Where you are a tenant in common, your share falls *within* your estate, and it must subsequently be distributed as per the wishes in your will.

Why Would I Choose Joint Tenancy?

Where you and your spouse both have equal access to tax relief, and you have every reason to believe that this situation will not change, you would purchase a property in joint names as joint tenants. The income from the property will be equally split between the two, as will the expenses and the tax deductions. On death, your share will revert to the other person, automatically. Where co-owners are joint tenants, each has an equal interest in the property, and no other agreement, either oral or in writing, can change this.

Borrowing as Joint Tenants

Joint tenants also become joint borrowers on any loan acquired for the purchase. You cannot be joint tenants but have one party get the loan for the entire purchase price to claim all of the tax benefits. While the bank may allow you to access a loan on a property in joint names with only one borrower, the tax department would not let that borrower claim all of the interest. They would consider that the borrower lent half of the money to the co-owner, and so the income and the expenses would be split anyway.

> Joint tenancy is the easiest way to apply for a loan...

Joint tenancy is the easiest way to apply for a loan as all acceptable income from all sources for all parties will be considered by the lender.

Tenants in Common

Buying an investment property as tenants in common with unequal shares has only just begun to be popular. This is because many marketers are convincing people that this is a legal way to maximise the tax benefits. But, this is only true where the parties can prove that they have a legitimate reason for having chosen to structure their property this way.

When you buy a property as tenants in common, you have paperwork prepared at the outset which declares the extent of your legal interest in the property. Legal interest is generally decided where another relationship already exists between the two parties which they wish to continue. For example, it could be that two people currently have a partnership agreement for another venture which sees one party owning 10% of the venture and the other 90%. These two parties may wish to continue in this manner, and so they decide to buy a property with a 90% share to one party and a 10% share to the other. As another example, two people may decide they would like to be 'in the business' of owing rental properties. Unlike the average investor, these two people may buy a portfolio of properties which they repair, manage and exert their own personal efforts to operate like a business. As these personal efforts may be exerted in different proportions, they could choose to set up as tenants in common with unequal legal shares in the business.

In both of these examples the parties have a legitimate reason for choosing a legal structure which results in an uneven division of the income and expenses, and the tax department would allow this.

Where two parties buy a property for the purposes of having an investment, there can be little reason why they would choose an unequal ownership split, unless it was so that one party could either avoid tax, or could claim a tax-deductible trip to inspect the property. Since neither of these reasons is legitimate, then despite the legal ownership, the tax department may disallow an unequal claim of income and expenses, unless the parties could prove other grounds for having chosen this unequal split.

This area of tax law is not only very vague but is certainly open to interpretation. While technically speaking you could make a claim for an unequal split of income and expenses if you had set up your tenancy in that way, if the tax department felt that you had only done so in order to purposefully avoid tax, then it may disallow the claim. It would certainly disallow a claim for travelling expenses for a 1% shareholder if you could prove no other reason for having structured your ownership in this manner.

Borrowing as Tenants in Common

Borrowing as tenants in common is exactly the same as borrowing as joint tenants. If your name is on the title, then you may become a borrower and your income can be considered when applying for the loan.

Whose Name?

In order to decide just who should buy the property, first work out where your cash flow is coming from. If it is coming from the tax relief because of a large, on-paper loss, then you will want to buy the property in the highest income earner's name. If the positive cash flow is because you have been lucky enough to find a property with a higher-than-average return for the price, and on-paper costs do not wipe out the gain, then you will want the property in the lowest income earner's name. If you are both in the same tax bracket, and you believe it will stay that way, then both should own the property.

An illustration will show the reasons for these decisions.

Michael earns $75,000 per annum, and Kathy earns $30,000. At present, they look like this:

Michael's income	$75,000	Kathy's income	$30,000
Michael's tax	$19,800	Kathy's tax	$4860
Net yearly Michael	$55,200	Net yearly Kathy	$25,140
Net weekly	$1,061.53	Net weekly	$483.46
Total weekly income for both:		**$1,544.99**	

The property they have found has an income of $12,000 a year, costs of $14,500 and depreciation in year one of $8,600.

If they buy the house in Kathy's name, this is how it will look:

For Tax

Kathy's income	$30,000
Rent	$12,000
Costs	$14,500
Depreciation	$8,600
Taxable income	$18,900
Tax payable	**$1,935**

Actual Cash Flow

Total income	$42,000
Costs to pay	$14,500
Tax to pay	$1,935
Net to Kathy	**$25,565**
	(or $492 a week)

In total, Kathy and Michael now have $1,553.53 a week, which is $8.54 more than they had without an investment.

If they were to buy in both names, it would look like this:

For Tax

Kathy's income	$30,000	*Michael's income*	$75,000
Rent	$6,000	*Rent*	$6,000
Costs	$7,250	*Costs*	$7,250
Depreciation	$4,300	*Depreciation*	$4,300
Taxable income	$24,450	*Taxable income*	$69,450
Tax payable	**$3,195**	Tax payable	**$17,469**

Actual Cash Flow

Total income	$117,000
Costs to pay	$14,500
Tax to pay	$20,664
Net to both	**$81,836**
	(or $1,573.76 a week)

In total, Kathy and Michael now have $1,573.76 a week, which is $20.23 more than they had with the investment in just Kathy's name, and $28.77 more than they had without an investment.

If they were to buy in Michael's name only, it would look like this:

For Tax

Michael's income	$75,000
Rent	$12,000
Costs	$14,500
Depreciation	$8,600
Taxable income	$63,900
Tax payable	**$15,138**

Actual Cash Flow

Total income	$87,000
Costs to pay	$14,500
Tax to pay	$15,138
Net to Michael	**$57,362**
	(or $1,103.11 a week)

In total, Kathy and Michael now have $1,586.57 a week, which is $12.81 more than they had with the investment in both names, and $41.58 more than they had without an investment.

Clearly, in this case the property is far better purchased in Michael's name only, as it will provide a greater cash flow, which in turn will provide a quicker acquisition of that vital equity, allowing leverage.

Where a property is positively geared, then the reverse will be true.

For example, take a property with income of $13,000, and costs of $10,000, but no depreciation benefits. The net gain is $3,000. For Kathy and Michael, the bottom lines will be:

1. In Kathy's name only, she will pay $900 more in tax.

2. In both names, they will pay a total of $1,155 more in tax.

3. In Michael's name only, he will pay $1,410 more in tax.

Where the property has more income than costs, but also has depreciation benefits, you will need to work out whether the property makes an on-paper gain, or an on-paper loss, before you decide in whose name to purchase. Destiny Finsoft can do these calculations at the touch of a button, so be sure to download your copy.

> Destiny Finsoft can do these calculations at the touch of a button, so be sure to download your copy.

What if My Structure is Wrong?

If you own property at present and you believe that the structure is wrong, there is very little you can do about it. To make any changes, you would have to technically 'purchase' or 'sell' your share of the property from or to the other party.

Even when you give your share of a property to a spouse, the receiving party must pay stamp duty on the value of the given portion as if it were a sale. The costs of making these alterations far outweigh the benefits. Far better to accept that you still have dozens of properties to buy, and you can even up the balance by being sure that future purchases are made wisely.

Structuring Your Borrowings

Chapter 9 looked at the different types of loans you can get when looking to buy property. In both that chapter and others, you have been shown the benefits of using a line of credit product, not only for its ability to help you to reduce your debt more quickly, but for its flexibility when using and managing the loan itself.

While most bank managers and brokers know that people like lines of credit, few of them are in a position to advise you on the best way to use your line of credit once you have it in place.

To get the most benefit and stay on the right side of the tax department, you must know how to manage your line of credit, and what you are allowed to do from the tax department's point of view. Let us look at how a typical line of credit may progress for an investor.

This line of credit commences by being a simple debt secured by one property, the owner-occupied home. A line of credit with a single 'account' is set up, and the borrower operates this line of credit as in Figure 11.1.

Figure 11.1

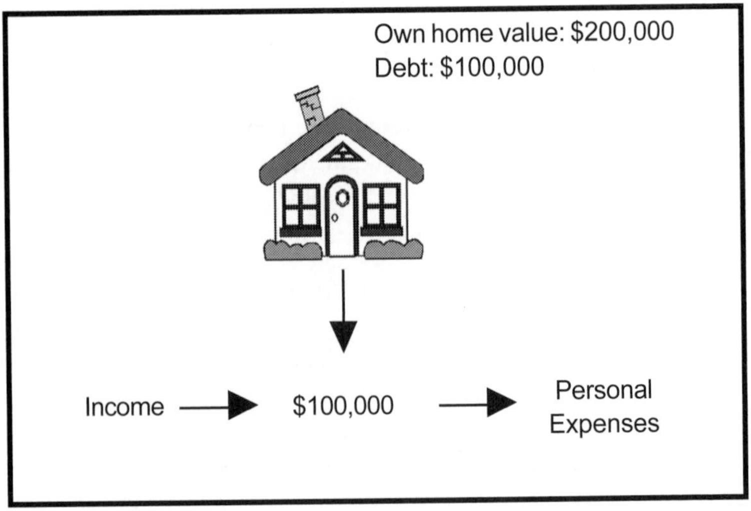

Own home value: $200,000
Debt: $100,000

Income ▶ $100,000 ▶ Personal Expenses

The client places all income into this loan and then draws out the expenses as and when they are needed. This will result in interest offsetting, and so reduce the balance of the loan at a quicker rate.

At present, this client already has the equity required to buy another property. So, he adds a property worth $150,000 (debt required $160,000) and splits the debt in two. Now it looks like Figure 11.2.

Figure 11.2

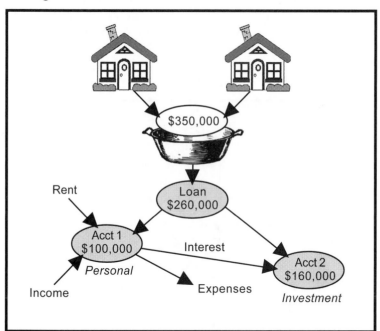

From this illustration, you can see that:

↪ The total loan is $260,000, which is a 75% loan-to-valuation ratio. In fact, the client would have qualified for $280,000 on equity, and most probably would have applied for this amount, leaving the extra amount as a buffer.

↪ Income from all sources goes into account 1 (personal debt).

↪ All expenses are paid from account 1, including property expenses, since the rent has been placed here.

↪ Interest is paid once a month to account 2 (investment debt). The tax department does not require investors to reduce this debt but it does not like it to increase or *capitalise*. (See the section on capitalising loans later in this chapter.)

After one year the personal debt (account 1) is paid down by 10% and values of both properties held have increased by 10%, making the owner-occupied home worth $220,000 and the existing investment property worth $165,000. The client can now add another property worth $150,000 (debt required $160,000— see Figure 11.3).

Figure 11.3

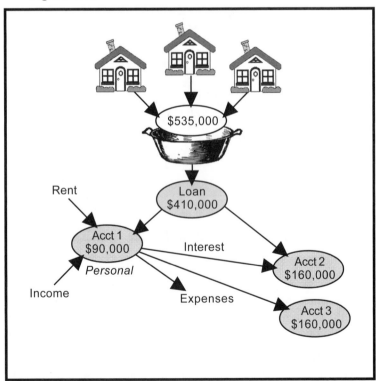

From this illustration, you can see that:

- ⮕ The property portfolio as a whole has gained equity. The repayments have come off the personal, non–tax-deductible debt (account 1) and the rising values of the properties helped to create even more equity.

- ⮕ The total loan is $410,000, which is a 76.6% loan-to-valuation ratio. In fact, the client would have qualified for $428,000 on equity.

- ⮕ Income from all sources still goes into account 1 (personal debt).

- ⮕ All expenses are paid from account 1, including property expenses.

- ⮕ The interest accrued on both of the investment accounts (2 & 3) is paid once a month.

Note here that although the equity (or deposit on the next property) initially becomes available in the personal account, because of the 'melting pot' it is shifted over to the investment account upon purchasing the property, ensuring that each investment property is in fact financed for 100% plus costs.

The investor could continue from here and the result would be that not only would the personal debt continue to decrease, but the speed with which properties could be purchased would increase as more properties were added. Oh, the power of leverage!

Saving Some Fees

For my own personal borrowing, I actually make things a little simpler.

While some people may like to keep a separate sub-account for each new property, I just lump mine all together into the one account. This saves me the fees on maintaining separate accounts, as usually a bank will charge an account-keeping fee on each one.

However, to do this you must keep accurate records on what proportion of the account is for each property. For example, when you buy the first property, 100% of the funds (and the interest) is attributable to that property. When you add the second property, depending on the purchase price, an amount of, say, 42% may be attributable to the first property while 58% is attributable to the second.

In keeping these accurate records you will enable your accountant to easily acquit your expenses for each property.

If you would rather be more compartmentalised than this, then take the separate accounts and pay the fees. They are usually not too high, anyway.

Using Other Banks

Sometimes you may wish to purchase a property which your current bank will not finance, possibly due to an internal policy (one you will most likely not understand!).

Under these circumstances, it is still possible to keep your current loan, create a deposit in an account with this bank, and simply take another loan with a different bank for the balance. Using the previous scenario, it may look like Figure 11.4.

> We will assume that another year has passed and all properties have risen by another 10%, making the values $242,000, $181,500 and $165,000, while the personal debt has reduced by another 10%. The investor wishes to buy another property for $150,000 but must go to another bank as this new property is out of policy for the current bank.

In this scenario, note that:

↪ The loan with the current bank is still only at a 75% loan-to-valuation ratio.

↪ The loan with the new bank is at an 80% loan-to-valuation ratio.

↪ The loan for the new property is represented by the $40,000 deposit with the first bank, and $120,000 with the second. Interest from both will add together and be tax deductible.

Figure 11.4

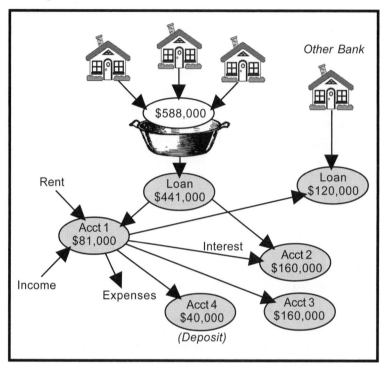

Although not ideal, this means that you still have the flexibility to go to another bank in the event that the one you are with cannot cater to your needs. Being flexible in this way will be very important if you are to have a variety of property in your portfolio, as you will find that policy regarding what a bank will accept as security will vary greatly from lender to lender.

Capitalising Your Loan

Some years ago people enjoyed the practice of setting up a scenario like the ones outlined in the illustrations on the previous pages, but did not make interest repayments to the investment loans. This could only be achieved where the borrowing capacity allowed the borrower to put in place a 'limit' which was higher than the actual balance of the drawings. This extra money then allowed people to go without paying the interest bill on their investment account, while still using all of the income from the investment to make payments to their personal account.

The result was that the investment account balance grew (as the interest was 'capitalised'), while the personal debt balance decreased at a very rapid rate. What was really happening here was that debt was being shifted from being personal, non–tax-deductible debt to being investment, tax-deductible debt. Since this debt grew, so did the amount of interest requiring payment (as interest was accruing on the interest), and so did the amount of tax you could get back.

While property salespeople still peddle this method of investment loan management, the tax department takes a dim view of capitalised loans. This is because in allowing your loan to capitalise, you are using the income from the property to obtain an extra, personal benefit, and the tax department does not allow you to claim a tax deduction where a personal benefit is obtained.

Having calculated the end result of capitalising a loan, it is useful to know that any benefit gained from capitalising an investment loan is usually lost, as the compounding interest results in less and less money in your own pocket. Better to stay on the right side of the tax office and at least meet your interest bill!

Conclusion

Consider carefully how you structure your investments. Also be aware that your personal circumstances can change rapidly. What worked for you five years ago may no longer be appropriate now, especially with the rules changing seemingly every five minutes.

Get some help from experts, but be sure that your own knowledge is kept up-to-date through your reading and by searching for new information from various websites and government offices. Don't forget that those emotions should be well and truly checked at the gate—this is a business and it deserves the same time and effort as any other business.

12 | Positive Cash Flow Property – Other Things You Should Know

➧ **Watch out for expensive 'courses'.**

➧ **Your aim when investing should be to work towards ownership.**

➧ **Be careful of getting advice from people who seem to make excessive money from that advice.**

➧ **Positive cash flow gives you not only the gain, but allows you to pay down your debt.**

IF YOU HAVE READ *How to Make Your Money Last as Long as You Do* and *How to Invest in Managed Funds*, then you will know that all of my books have a chapter in which I include bits and pieces which I would really like you to know about, but which do not seem to fit anywhere else!

You see, when I write a book I start at the beginning and as I progress, I keep a piece of paper nearby where I write all of the thoughts which pop into my head as I am writing. As I use each thought I cross it off the list. When I get to the end, sure enough there are still a dozen or so thoughts which just did not fit into any particular chapter.

So here we are at that point where you are (hopefully) very excited about your financial future, and you have obtained the information you need to make wise choices for prudent investing. Let us have a look at those extra little bits and pieces which may just help you along the way.

The Point

The information contained in this chapter is not considered vital in your investment strategy—however it may just answer those few remaining questions which you might have.

Making a Negative Cash Flow Property Positive

Many readers of my first book were so motivated by the information contained therein that they emailed to ask me what they could do about the property they currently had which had a negative cash flow.

In most cases, the answer is—nothing. Well, that is not entirely true, because if you can work hard on the debt and reduce the interest bill on the borrowings, eventually a negatively geared property will become positively geared and you will begin to see a gain on which you will pay tax.

However, if you have a personal, non–tax-deductible debt, you will not want to pay-off investment debt, otherwise you will simply make your tax position even less appealing.

Of course, you can go and find a strong positive cash flow property, which should then provide you with the cash flow to meet the shortfall in your negatively geared property. This would at least mean that you are not paying from your own pocket and your position would be neutral until you could add more property.

Another method is to add some furniture. The extra costs of adding this furniture (which extends to the added interest on the loan) may make the property positive cash flow.

> Belinda bought a property with a value of $150,000. The income would be $8,840 a year, and the costs of the loan ($160,000 at 6.25%), would be $10,000. Other costs would total $2,000. She has capital works deductions of $2,000 a year.

Belinda's position would be as follows:

↪ Her on-paper loss is $5,160.

↪ Her tax saving (in the 42% tax bracket) is $2,167.

↪ Her actual income is $11,007 ($8,840 in rent and $2,167 tax savings).

↪ Her actual expenses are $12,000.

↪ The loss to Belinda is $993, or $19 a week.

> When Belinda bought this property, she decided to furnish it. She purchased furniture to the value of $12,000, by increasing her loan to $172,000. This furniture enabled her to obtain $15 a week more in income, making the income $9,620. It also meant that she had to pay $750 a year more in interest, making her interest bill $10,750. Her furniture had a range of varying 'effective lives', but let's say that this averaged 20% a year. This means that, in addition to the capital works deductions, she could also claim $2,400 a year in depreciation.

Belinda's position is now as follows:

↪ Her on-paper loss is $7,790.

↪ Her tax saving (in the 42% tax bracket) is $3,271.

↪ Her actual income is $12,891 ($9,620 in rent and $3,271 tax savings).

↪ Her actual expenses are $12,750.

↪ The gain to Belinda is $141, or $2.70 a week.

In Belinda's case, this was an effective strategy for eliminating the negative cash flow. But there are a few things to note about using this pathway:

1. Belinda was able to obtain a higher loan because she had enough equity in existing property. If the purchase price of the new property means that you will already be

committed to a loan-to-valuation ratio of 80%, then the
bank will not let you borrow any more (without lender's
mortgage insurance). Even where a furniture pack is
included in the price of a property, banks will not lend
against furniture, and will reduce the price against which
they will base their loan to you by the value of the
furniture (meaning they will lend 80% of the price after
the value of the furniture is deducted).

2. If Belinda was in a lower tax bracket this strategy would not
    have eliminated the loss entirely.

3. Furnished properties are not always a good idea. It depends
    greatly on where you buy the property. For example, my
    property in Cairns is furnished. This is because Cairns has
    an itinerant population (with most people on a working
    holiday), and being so far north many people choose not to
    bring furniture with them. On the other hand, a property I
    have in NSW is leased to long-term tenants who prefer to
    use their own furniture. Having this property furnished
    would only make it harder to let.

You may be lucky enough to have not yet acquired any
properties. If this is you, then be sure to always accept only
properties with a positive cash flow, and you will not have this
problem to deal with!

Won't the Property Lose Tax Advantages as the Loan is Reduced?

Sometimes, the desire to be sure that the tax department does
not get its hands on too much of our money overcomes our
common sense.

In Chapter 11, we looked at the strategy an investor must use
to reduce borrowings. This strategy involved gaining equity in
your loans—paying them off in fact. Once your personal debt
is finalised, you will want to begin to pay-off your investment
debts.

I am often asked if it is wise to pay-off an investment loan because then you lose the tax deductibility status. Yes, you do. And yes, this is what you want. You *want* to pay tax. The more tax you pay, the more you must be earning!

This is not to say that you try to pay tax when you do not have to! It simply means that your aim when investing should be to work towards ownership, as only through ownership can you continue to increase your portfolio.

Usually, when people buy negatively geared property, the cash flow is negative at the beginning, and over a number of years this position changes. Once you begin to pay down the debt, and as rents rise with inflation, your income will gradually exceed your expenses and you will find that the negatively geared property becomes positively geared.

> The more tax you pay, the more you must be earning!

If you buy positive cash flow, the same thing will happen. The difference is:

↪ Your negatively geared property started by showing a loss, and then eventually made a gain, resulted in additional tax.

↪ Your positive cash flow property gave you money from day one and, since much of the loss is on paper, should stay in an on-paper loss situation *longer*, lengthening the time until you begin to pay tax, without affecting the speed with which you gain equity. In fact, you will gain equity more quickly as the positive cash flow pays off principal.

Eric bought a property with a first-year income of $10,000 and expenses of $13,000. Being in the 30% tax bracket, he had to foot $2,100 of this bill.

Eric paid approximately $5,000 a year off this debt (since he had no personal debt), and his rent return rose by 3% a year.

Eric's position progressed as shown on the following page (assuming 6.25% on the loan and no inflation on expenses).

Year	$ Loss/Gain
1	−2,100
2	−1,670
3	−1,233
4	−795
5	−347
6	+154

From this illustration, we see that Eric's loss continues for five years, and in the sixth year he will begin to pay tax. In total, Eric loses $6,145 before he begins to make any gain.

> Kristy buys a property with a first-year income of $10,000, expenses of $13,000, and depreciation and capital works deductions totalling an average of $7,800 a year. Being in the 30% tax bracket, she has a positive cash flow in year one of $254.

> Kristy paid approximately $5,000 a year off this debt (since she had no personal debt), and her rent return rose by 3% a year.

Kristy's position progressed as follows (assuming 6.25% on the loan and no inflation on expenses):

Year	$ Loss/Gain
1	+254
2	+669
3	+1,107
4	+1,545
5	+1,992
6	+2,447
7	+2,909

The major points to note are:

- ➥ Despite the gain, Kristy is not paying tax—this gain is coming from the tax not paid due to an on-paper loss.

- ➥ After six years she has already made $8,014, putting her $14,159 ahead of Eric.

- ➥ If we were to assume that the depreciation went on in this manner, Kristy would not be in a tax-payable position until year 16.

- ➥ After five years the depreciation would reduce to mostly just capital works deductions (as most depreciable plant items have an effective life of around five years), which would mean that Kristy would not be in a tax-payable position until year 12.

Just in case the rest of this book has not convinced you that positive cash flow property has myriad benefits, this example should. Positive cash flow gives you not only the gain, but allows you to pay down your debt (creating equity), while still maintaining tax advantages for many years!

Is Tourism Property Better?

The answer to this question is yes. And no.

Tourism property has benefits, but it can also have drawbacks. The major benefit of tourism property is that the capital works deduction allowed is 4% per annum, rather than 2.5%. Although this is only allowed for a shorter time (25 years rather than 40), by the time 25 years have elapsed you will most likely be retiring and not be so worried about these deductions.

Another benefit is that very often tourism property can have pooled income, and for a successful property this can be a boon for investors (see Chapter 3). Where the area you have chosen is very popular, you can make much more money on the rent return than you could ever hope to with standard residential property due to the high occupancy. And, where there are periods of low occupancy, these periods of high occupancy can sustain you through the lean times.

On the negative side, tourism is very cyclical. A popular destination this year may be the place every one stays away from next year. It can be prone to many outside economic factors over and above those affecting the rental market, such as a slowdown in tourism and high inflation. And the seasonal nature of travel may mean that you have to more carefully manage your cash flow, putting aside the profits from the high times to pay costs in the low times.

However, as part of a balanced portfolio, and if chosen with thought and research, tourism property can certainly enhance your position very nicely. As with all investing, I would advise anyone considering a tourism investment to ensure that, eventually, their portfolio has a mix of all property.

The Procrastinator

This section is for those people who would dearly love to invest in property, yet find that they are being held back by an invisible hand, a little voice telling them that it is just not safe.

For those of my personal clients who fall into this category—you know who you are! In case you are not sure, if you are a procrastinator, you will:

- Read a lot of books about investing.
- Get very motivated and tell yourself that *this* is the year.
- Watch others get ahead and just know that you should be doing so too.
- Get lots of information sent to you about possible investments.
- Draw up a list with dozens of inconsequential 'problems' with the investment and focus on these, ignoring the dozens of *huge* benefits.
- Possibly even make further enquiries and get very close to closing the sale.
- Find that, at the last minute the cat dies, the car breaks down, the butcher advises against it or a relatively minor glitch in the sale makes you skittish and you breathe a sigh of relief and back out.

For all of these people, let me reassure you of a few things:

1. You will not die if you go ahead.

2. People like myself are here to help you and to give you the best possible chance of succeeding.

3. The first one is by far the hardest. From there, it becomes a breeze.

4. It's like having a baby. It might hurt like crazy but look what you get in the end!

5. If it all goes to pieces tomorrow, then what have you really lost? Probably nothing, and at least you tried. Incidentally, I have yet to meet someone who has had it really go to pieces so much that nothing could be salvaged.

Don't make any more excuses. Hold your breath and jump. Make yourself proceed. You are getting older every second of the day. You are getting closer to retirement. And, I can promise you one thing; retirement is a *very* long time to be without money, especially if your health also fades. If you do not start today, you will be one of those poor unfortunates, living on the poverty line just waiting to go to the big retirement home in the sky!

Lines of Credit and Mortgage Reduction

By now you should be quite familiar with accelerated mortgage reduction. You only need to visit the local shopping centre to find a slick looking salesperson with a little table, asking you if you want to save $100,000 on your mortgage.

Accelerated mortgage reduction simply involves getting a line of credit loan, and paying all income into this loan as soon as it is earned. While this income sits and offsets interest (as interest accrues on your daily balance), you cleverly use a credit card (one with reward points, of course), to pay all of your bills. You then must make sure that you draw back from your line of credit in time to pay-off the credit card and avoid paying interest on it. In doing this, you have hit the bank with a double whammy. You have *saved* interest on your mortgage, while using the banks money, free of charge, to pay your bills.

You don't need to pay someone thousands of dollars to give you this idea and to set up the loan for you. But you do need to follow a system of some sort and have support for it to really work for you.

My company writes a lot of loans for one particular bank (the one with what I consider to be the best line of credit, of course). Last week one of the managers was telling me how a lot of people were regretting getting a line of credit as they had not managed it well, and that in his opinion one day the banks would stop offering them (sure they will—the bank *wants* you to stay fully drawn on your line of credit!). I asked him to look over the balances of the loans in our quite substantial 'loan book'. In the entire book, only one loan was in arrears, and this was because the client still had not worked out that they needed to make an interest payment each month (we were working hard with this client!).

> Mortgage reduction simply will not work for you without these vital ingredients.

This is not an accident. This is because all of our clients are following a system. And of those clients who diligently follow their personalised system, all find that after a few years they are in fact well ahead of where they expected to be.

How to Make Your Money Last as Long as You Do made a distinction between a 'spender' and an investor' (recommended reading if you have not already done so).

If you are a spender, then do not get a line of credit. And, if you intend to pay someone for the privilege of assisting you to reduce your mortgage, be very sure that they can offer you a complete and personalised system which includes regular acquisition of positive cash flow property. Mortgage reduction simply will not work for you without these vital ingredients.

Watch Out for Expensive 'Courses'

I am horrified at the number of 'experts' around today who charge unbelievable sums for investors to attend courses designed to assist them to amass millions of dollars worth of property. The theory is that, since you will learn how to become a millionaire quickly, then you should be prepared to commit some $20,000 or so for the privilege of learning how.

Well, luckily for you, at this point you have only committed around 0.1% of that amount to buy this book, and you have received far more honest and legitimate information than these courses will ever provide.

I know people who have been to these courses, and I have been able to view some of the material. While I admit that perhaps 3% of the population would be willing to take the very large risks these people are suggesting, the techniques covered simply do not work much of the time.

Without being specific about the actual course, here are a few common techniques suggested by these people which probably will not work out for you, or may even be illegal.

1. Buying Off-the-Plan with Multiple Deposit Bonds

This technique calls for the investor to find four or five properties yet to be built and secure these properties by using deposit bonds (which cost around 10% of what an actual deposit would cost you). The theory is that you will be able to buy these properties cheaper as they are 'off the plan'. You will then sell them prior to settlement (which is usually 12 to 18 months hence) for a profit, and pocket the difference.

The problems here are:

- You must have finance approved to get a deposit bond.

- Most banks will want to know about any 'pending loans' you may have elsewhere. You must disclose these. If you do, then you may have no borrowing capacity left. If you don't, then you are committing mortgage fraud

- If you get to settlement and cannot sell the properties, you must proceed. If you have no deposit or not enough equity in other property, you will not be able to proceed and so you will be sued by the vendor.

- If you sell at the same price you paid (or less) then you are out of pocket.

2. Buying Off-the-Plan at a Lower-Than-Market Price

The idea here is that you go to a developer and offer to buy, say, five of the properties they have on the market, getting a discount for the bulk purchase. You then apply to the bank for a loan of 80% (or 90%) of the *market* value which, since you got a discount, should actually end up covering the entire purchase price.

The main problem with this one is that market price is determined by what someone will pay for a property, not by the asking price. So, if you lived in a block of flats with apartments valued at $180,000, and your desperate neighbours sold their apartment for $160,000, then $160,000 becomes the market price.

Most lenders will lend an amount which is a percentage of *market* value, not purchase price, so this will mean that it may be very hard to find a lender to provide the funds you need.

3. Buying a Property Which Needs Work, Doing a Budget
Make-Over and Selling it for a $50,000 Profit

Yes, I know they do it on TV all the time. And if I was that clever (and had oodles of time) perhaps I could do it too.

The truth is, in most cases, cosmetic renovations on a property add only to saleability, rarely to price. I often go to the homes of clients who have just spent $10,000 on painting and decorating. They are disappointed when this does not add $10,000 (or even $20,000) to the value of their home.

In reality, even adding an entirely new room will rarely add even the actual cost of the room to the property. Valuations are based on the size of the house and the area in which it is built.

> ...cosmetic renovations on a property add only to saleability, rarely to price.

If you do buy a property needing work, it is highly likely you will find that, after the purchasing and sale costs, the cost of the materials and the notional cost of the time you have spent (I don't know about you, but I put a pretty high value on my time!), it is most unlikely that you will even get back what you have spent.

4. Putting in a Low Offer and then Bribing the Valuer to Send in a High Valuation

Of course, the course presenters do not call it bribing! Here the method involves getting to the valuer and convincing him or her to return to the bank a valuation higher than what you are actually paying. In the event that the lender will lend on valuation rather than purchase price, this results in enough money to buy the property without having to use any of your own money.

It does not take a genius to identify the problem here! In case you didn't already know, valuers work for the bank, not for the investor! Most valuers who I know are straight and honest. Even I couldn't sweet-talk them into providing higher valuations (not that I have tried). And, if you upset a valuer too much by trying this, he or she may knock a few thousand off the purchase price, just to show you!

Be very careful of these kinds of courses. The only people getting rich from them are the course presenters. And, I am sure that it will not be too long until we begin to see the damage these people are really causing, in the form of the poor people who find themselves in trouble from trying out their techniques. However, do not under-estimate the importance of education—there are courses which do offer value for money and action plans which can work in practice.

Renting Out the Property You Move From

When you have lived in a house for a long time, you naturally become attached to it. So much so that many people have this romantic notion of keeping the house from which they have moved, as it would make a 'good' investment.

Aside from this being a very emotional thought, there are real reasons why this is not a good plan.

> Denise and Todd have lived in their home for 12 years. They only owe $50,000, and it is now valued at $250,000. They would like to move but think that their home would make a

good investment property, as it will fetch $280 a week ($14,560 a year). It will only have costs of $2,000 a year.

They apply to the bank to borrow $315,000 to buy their dream home ($300,000 plus costs). The bank has two securities (totalling $550,000) so it will lend Denise and Todd the $365,000 in total ($50,000 for their current home and $315,000 for their new home) which they need to move. The interest rate is 6.25%.

The position for Denise and Todd is:

↝ Their personal debt has an interest bill of $19,687.50 a year, with no tax benefits.

↝ The investment debt has an interest bill of $3,125 a year.

↝ They will make a yearly gain on the investment property of $9,435. Since the property is in both names, then this gain is split. Denise pays $1,415.25 tax on her share of the gain (at 30%) while Todd pays $1,981.35 tax on his share (at 42%).

↝ Their total outlay for this exercise is $13,649.10 ($19,687.50 + $3,125 + $2,000 + 1,415.25 + $1,981.35 − $14,560).

Louise and Greg have also lived in their home for 12 years. They only owe $50,000, and it is now valued at $250,000. They would like to move, so they sell their home, realising $242,000 from the sale (a net of $192,000 after repaying their debt).

They apply to the bank to borrow $123,000 to buy their dream home which will cost them $315,000 in total, of which they have $192,000. In addition, they borrow a further $260,000, in Greg's name only, to buy an investment property worth $250,000.

The bank has two securities (totalling $550,000) so it will lend Louise and Greg the $383,000 in total which they need to move and buy a new investment property. The interest rate is 6.25%.

↪ Their personal debt has an interest bill of $7,687 a year, with no tax benefits.

↪ The investment debt has an interest bill of $16,250 a year.

↪ They will make a loss on the investment property of $3,690 (considering all is equal, and the property is negatively geared). Since the property is in one name, then this loss is applied to Greg's tax. He gets back $1,549.80 in tax.

↪ Their total outlay for this exercise is $9,827.20 ($7,687 + $16,250 + $2,000 – $1,549.80 – $14,560).

In actual fact, Louise and Greg would have been smart enough to buy a positive cash flow property. If this were the case, then they would have even more positive cash flow, reducing their net cost further. You can see from this illustration that net cash flow is a very big reason not to keep the house you move from.

Other reasons are more emotional. Could you really stand to watch someone else possibly not take care of a house you have grown to love? If it is no longer right for you to live in, then you should have no attachment to it. Cut the heartstrings and move on—your bank balance will thank you in the end.

Buying an Investment Property While you are on Holidays

The sun is shining, you are relaxed and you are strolling along the golden sands of paradise beach. A flyer blows through the air and you grab it, to find an enticing advertisement seeking investors to share in the glories that paradise can offer.

Why not? You love the place, you are more relaxed than you have been for a long time so surely others will feel the same?

No, they may not. Making a hard business decision is not possible in such an idyllic setting. Go home, get back to work, immerse yourself in the stresses that life has to offer, and then think again. Do the sums, and if it still looks good in the cold hard light of day, then it may be a possibility after all.

Property Traders

I truly admire people with the time and knack to take perfectly awful properties and make them a 'house and garden' showpiece. This kind of transformation takes not only time and creativity, but usually a lot of money.

> Buying properties and doing them up for sale and a quick profit is not always the money-spinner it appears.

There are a small handful of people who make a living out of restoring derelict properties for profit. Even these professionals still take a risk, and it does not always work out profitably for them.

Buying properties and doing them up for sale and a quick profit is not always the money-spinner it appears. If this is what you would like to do, then the principles outlined in this book may not be right for you. And, since it costs so much in this country to buy and sell, it is not likely that you will make any grand profits from the exercise.

Conclusion

Without goals, plans can never be made. Without vision, goals can never be realised. If a self-supported retirement is what you truly want, then the steps have been provided for you here in these pages.

Be careful of getting advice from people who seem to make excessive money from that advice with little support offered. Seek out professionals to help you who know their business and can provide to you a system to follow and a pathway to success. Take advice from those who have a right to provide it—your mechanic might be a nice guy but he cannot give you advice about investing, nor can your next-door neighbour or one of your well-meaning relatives.

Become educated about investing and soon you will be the expert—but remember that knowing about a subject does not qualify you as an expert unless you practice what you preach. Read and learn, and get ready to start as soon as you can.

13 | The Journey

➠ **If property is the vehicle of your choice, then you cannot afford to buy anything other than positive cash flow property.**

➠ **Knowing what type of property to buy is the first step.**

➠ **There has never been a better time to provide a wonderful future for yourself than this very minute!**

A JOURNEY OF A thousand miles starts with just one small step. Rome wasn't built in a day. Look before you leap.

I am full of marvellous cliches, I know—but there is one thing I am sure of. While you need the courage of your convictions to invest, you do not need to be a genius, a risk-taker or otherwise possessed of any special skill. You just need to be careful, informed and prepared to ask the right questions of the right people.

Having made it right through this book, your head will be buzzing and, I hope, your heart will be racing with excitement. Before you rush headlong into looking for positive cash flow property, let me summarise the things you should know, and direct you back to the right section if you are still unsure of any small thing.

Step 1

How do you know if you are ready to invest? Being aware of the real risks of investing can help you identify if you are prepared to take those risks. Once you have identified these risks, you will need to know whether you are ready financially. Investing too early can be worse than investing too late, as you may run the risk of becoming over-exposed. To be sure that you fully understand the risks, and to know if you are ready to invest, go back and review Chapter 1.

Step 2

So many people today are espousing the benefits of investing in property, yet few really understand the difference between positive cash flow and negative gearing. You may have heard about positively geared property, but in reality true positive cash flow property can be hard to recognise, unless you know what to look for. Positive cash flow property provides all of the benefits that negative gearing brings, without costing you money from your pocket each week.

If property is the vehicle of your choice, then you cannot afford to buy anything other than positive cash flow property. If you are still unsure of what this really is, read Chapter 2 again.

Step 3

When you buy property, it is just as important to obtain balance within your portfolio as it is with any other investment. While investing across a wide range of assets has been proven to be the most effective way to invest, some people feel safer sticking to just property. If this is you, you will need to know more about the different kinds of property available, so that you may fill your portfolio with a wide range and so expose yourself evenly across many property types. Chapter 3 provided many great examples of different types of property, and also assessed these choices in terms of their relative risk to each other, and to other asset classes.

> Investing too early can be worse than investing too late...

Step 4

Knowing what type of property to buy may be the first step, but knowing where to find it can be a little more difficult. As owners of residential property many of us feel capable of making the choice on our own. All too often emotions get in the way and we end up making mistakes with our choice.

There are basic features which make a property a 'good' investment, and none of them relate to the physical appearance of the property. For a complete outline of what makes a property a viable possibility, have another look at Chapter 4.

Step 5

An effective investment is one which provides us with the opportunity to hedge against adverse events. Where an investment relies on outside events to remain static for it to make a gain, it is likely that this inflexibility will result in loss over time.

Positive cash flow property can provide an effective hedge against inflation, rising interest rates and an under-supply of tenants, as well as times of low occupancy. In addition, a property which has a positive cash flow allows the investor to leverage at a greater rate. The ability to leverage from one investment to the next is where true investing power is seen. If you want to revise the hedging and leveraging benefits of positive cash flow property, revisit Chapter 5.

Step 6

Whenever you choose to invest, you are well-advised to carry out the required due diligence. Most investors attend to this rigorously where share or managed fund investments are involved. Yet, when it comes to property too many investors rely on their own instincts, or on the information provided by the salesperson concerned. Knowing the questions to ask is an important factor here, and you may be surprised to find that the questions required are nothing like those you would ask if you were seeking owner-occupied housing. For a complete list of the right questions, take another look at Chapter 6.

Step 7

Wise investors know that a good spread of property may well involve investing out of your home state. Unfortunately, real estate law is state law, and this means that no two states in Australia have the same process for purchasing property. If you have decided to spread your wings and invest in a state with which you are unfamiliar, Chapter 7 outlines for you all of the different rules of conveyancing for each state. It will also provide information about other tools which you may need to use when buying property.

Step 8

Once you have purchased an investment property, you will become a landlord. Unless you have been one before, this experience can be fraught with problems, which are easy to rectify if you know what you are doing.

> Being fully informed about lending is a vital step...

Some landlords choose to manage a property themselves. This is more likely to be a false economy. Property management is usually a job which is best left to the professionals. To know more about your responsibilities as a landlord, and how to select a property manager, go back to Chapter 8.

Step 9

Borrowing to buy property is an important part of your investment strategy and one which will increase your capacity to acquire property. Yet too many investors are careless, and do not research the loans they are offered. This can result in you being provided with a loan which limits your future borrowing, or in some other way impacts negatively on your plans. Being fully informed about lending is a vital step covered in Chapter 9.

Step 10

Investing in real estate carries with it substantial taxation benefits. Few professionals are fully informed as to the true extent of these benefits, leaving it to the taxpayer to find out for themselves. To avoid costly mistakes which may be hard to rectify, be sure to completely read Chapter 10 to fully understand your tax position.

Step 11

All too often investors do not realise the impact of a poorly structured investment. If you are careful, the right structure can often result in a far more tax-effective investment. In addition, while the type of loan is important to your investment, so is the way you subsequently arrange and manage that loan. Before proceeding with any property purchase, be sure you have read and understood Chapter 11.

Step 12

As a final step, be sure to read all of the little hints and tips contained in Chapter 12. These hints may clear up any remaining questions you may have and could well save you making costly mistakes.

Be sure to email us at Destiny Financial Solutions so that you can download your copy of the free software. It is an excellent tool which will help to make your investing that much more simple.

> ...don't put off until tomorrow what you can do today...

Ask for help along the way—while you must be clever about how you invest you do not have to be so clever that you need to do it yourself. Having knowledgeable advisers and continuous education is imperative. Following a system will keep you on the track towards success.

I help dozens of people every week from all walks of life and from every level of income, and I don't believe any of them are not clever! They simply appreciate that their own expertise is limited to what they are good at, and they are not afraid to ask for help.

And lastly, as my mother always told me, don't put off until tomorrow what you can do today—because tomorrow never comes. There has never been a better time to provide a wonderful future for yourself than this very minute!

Glossary

Adjustment   The apportion at settlement of expenses like water rates and council rates between the buyer and vendor.

Bond   An amount of money paid by the tenant and held in trust to cover any damage at the end of a rental period.

Capital costs   Costs incurred when purchasing a property as well as those paid for structural improvements.

Capital gain   The profit made on an investment.

Capital loss   The loss made on an investment.

Capital works deductions   The amount of depreciation which can be claimed on the construction costs of an investment property.

Caveat   Any person with a legal interest in a property can lodge a caveat with the Titles Office to ensure the property is not sold without his or her knowledge. A property cannot be transferred from one party to another while a caveat is in place.

Certificate of Title   Legal proof of ownership of a property, carrying the owner's name and other information.

Chattels   Personal property, buildings and fixtures or clothes, furniture, and other items within a property.

Commission (real estate)   Fee payable to a real estate agent (or other salesperson) for selling a property by the person authorising the sale. Usually a percentage of the sale price, or can be a set fee where a relationship between the developer and salesperson exists.

Common property   Areas in strata-titled properties shared and maintained by all owners.

Community title   Title where the land component is owned by a group with rights for an individual to build on a portion of that land.

Company title   This title applies when owners of flats in a block form a company. Each has shares in the company which owns the land and buildings. The owner of the shares is entitled to exclusive occupation of a flat.

Contract of Sale   Written agreement setting out the terms and conditions of a property sale.

Conveyancing   Legal process of transferring the ownership of a property from one person to another. Can be carried out by either a property solicitor, a conveyancer or a settlement agent.

Cooling-Off   The period after signing a purchase contract in which you may withdraw from the purchase.

Covenant   Conditions affecting the use of land or property which are written into the title.

Deposit   Usually 5% to 10% of the purchase price of a property placed in trust upon exchange or signing of the contract.

Deposit bond   An insurance policy guaranteeing a purchaser's deposit in the event of a contract default.

Depreciation   Where the original cost of an item is progressively written off over its effective life.

Easement   Right of way which may run through your property.

Equity   The difference between what you owe and what you own.

Fittings and fixtures   Items such as baths, stoves, lights and other fittings, kitchen, linen or storage cupboards or wardrobes. Fittings are not normally included in a contract if they can be removed without causing damage.

Freehold   An owner's interest in a property.

General Law Title (Old Title)   Old, complicated form of land ownership in the form of a chain of documents.

Interest-only loans   A loan on which interest only is paid periodically and the principal is paid at the end of the term.

Inventory   List of items included with a property for sale.

Investment   The purchase of a security with the ultimate goal of producing capital gain or an income.

Joint tenants   Joint tenancy is the equal holding of property by two or more persons.

Land tax   Value-based levy applied to some property. Varies from state to state.

Landlord   The owner of an investment property.

Lease   A document granting possession of a property for a given period without conferring ownership. The lease document specifies the terms and conditions of occupancy by the tenant.

Maturity   The last day of the term of a loan or the day an investment is realised.

Mortgage   Legal agreement on the terms and conditions of a loan for the purpose of buying real estate, whereby the person offering the mortgage takes security over property.

Mortgagee   The bank or lender who lends the money for the property.

Mortgagor   One who borrows the money to purchase property.

Multiple listing   System of selling the property through many agents. The buyer pays only one commission.

Negative gearing   The writing off of investment property losses where a negative cash flow results—i.e. expenses exceed income.

Offer and acceptance   A formal legal agreement which offers a specified price for a specified property. The offer may be firm (no conditions attached) or have special conditions.

Old System Title   Property title whereby the chain of ownership is established.

Opportunity cost   The notional cost whereby money is lost by not investing in an opportunity.

Owner-occupied   Property in which the owners reside—that is, non–income-producing property.

Plan   This shows the ground plan design, elevation of house, number and size of rooms, kitchen, bathrooms and laundry layout, position of the house on the land, etc.

Positive gearing   Where income on an investment property exceeds expenses and tax must be paid on the gain.

Principal   The original amount of money that has been borrowed not considering accruing interest.

Private sale   The seller does not engage an estate agent but acts on his or her own behalf.

Private treaty sale   Sale of property via an agent through private negotiation and contract.

Real property   Land, with or without improvements.

Requisition of title   The process in which the buyer of a property asks for written information about the title to a property from the vendor in addition to that supplied in the Contract of Sale.

Reserve price   Price below which an owner is not prepared to sell at auction.

Revenue costs   Costs incurred to earn income on an investment property.

Security   Property offered to the mortgagee in return for a loan.

Settlement   Completion of sale (or advancing of a loan) when the balance of a contract price is paid to the vendor and the buyer is legally entitled to take possession of the property.

Shares   Unit of ownership in a publicly listed company, which can be traded on the stock exchange.

Sole agency One agent or agency has the sole rights to sell a property.

Stamp duty A state government tax imposed on the sale of real estate.

Strata title Most commonly used for flats and units, this title gives you ownership of a small piece of a larger property and includes common property.

Survey Confirmation of the property boundaries and improvements.

Tenancy in common Tenancy in common is the holding of property by two or more persons, with either equal shares or unequal shares. If one person dies, the property is dealt with in accordance with the will.

Term The time length of a loan.

Title search The process of examining the land title to ensure the vendor has the right to sell and therefore transfer ownership.

Torrens title System of recording ownership of property, also known as Certificate of Title. Most common and simplest form of title to property.

Transfer Document registered in the Land Titles Office recording change of ownership of a property.

Unencumbered Property free of covenants or other restrictions.

Valuation Assessment of the value of a property given in a written report by a registered valuer.

Variable rate loan A home loan for which the interest rate changes as the money market changes.

Vendor Person offering a property for sale.

Vendor statement Statement setting out particulars of the property, made by the vendor.

Index

property laws
—Australian Capital
Territory 102
—New South Wales 99-100
—Northern Territory 102
—Queensland 103-104
—South Australia 102
—Tasmania 104
—Victoria 100-101
—Western Australia 102-103
property
—clubs 63
—developers 6, 62-63
—inspecting 51, 94-95
—maintenance 128
—managers 37, 42, 92,
115-116, 119-121
—monitoring 52-53
—purchasing 93, 97-99,
188-191
—syndicates 43-45
—trusts 43-45
—value 10, 11

R

renovations 10, 89-90, 210
rent 21-22, 56-59, 70-71,
117, 123-124
—guarantee 92-93
repairs 125, 127
research 55, 111
residential property 32-35
—benefits of 33
resorts 40
responsible entity 40, 92
retirement 2, 15
returns 6, 20, 21-23
risk 3-10, 8-9, 32
—comparison 6-7, 35, 36,
39, 43, 45
—profile 8-9

S

saleability 10
seminars 14, 77
sinking fund 91
sole owner 184-185
solicitors 105-109
success 7-8
superannuation 2

T

tax 20, 127, 163-182, 202-
204
—and investing 167-170
—deductions 35, 41
—rates 23
—variation request 29
tenancy agreements 121-124
tenant damage 9, 118
tenants 9, 88, 113, 115-116,
120
tenants in common 187-188
titles
—old system 33
—strata 33
—Torrens 33
tourism property 36-43, 92,
205-206
—features of 38-39, 41-42
transport 89
travel costs 128-129, 177

V

vacancy 9, 69-70, 87
vacant land 35
valuer 10

1. Investment seminars

Margaret Lomas frequently conducts evening seminars around the country. The aim of the seminars is to provide clarity on information contained in Margaret's books and to allow attendees the chance to have their personal questions answered. To find out about the next seminar in your state, visit **www.destiny.net.au** or phone **1800 648 640**.

Watch the website for more information about all Destiny® events.

2. Personal support and assistance

Destiny® Financial Solutions is expanding its network to provide personal assistance by trained branch staff in many areas throughout Australia. We can assist you to put together a personalised property investing strategy that is not reliant on the purchase of a particular property. All of our branches offer financial advising support and assistance for direct property investors. Phone or email us, or visit the website to find out our branch locations or to ask about the unique services we can offer.

To discover more, visit **www.destiny.net.au**

3. Free download — Destiny® FinSoft

All readers qualify for this unique program which calculates cash flow for you and provides an abundance of other calculators and useful website links.

Phone **1800 648 640** or for email instructions contact: **download@destiny.net.au**

4. Join the Destiny® team

Do you possess a passion for property investment and have a genuine interest in helping others to achieve their financial goals?

Destiny® Financial Solutions is an innovative national company that has carved out a unique position in the financial services landscape.

A pioneer of the property investment industry, Destiny® assists clients to achieve prosperity using direct residential property as the vehicle.

With massive plans for further growth, we are looking for the right people to play their part in our future success.

At Destiny®, we are committed to:

- absolute integrity in all client dealings
- a culture of ethics and honesty
- a people-first attitude
- making a positive contribution to the community.

Would you make an outstanding participant in a business opportunity based on these philosophies?

For more information on business opportunities offered by Destiny® visit our website at **www.destiny.net.au**. Alternatively, you can email Destiny® Managing Director Reuben Lomas on **reuben.lomas@destiny.net.au**

Thank you for reading this book. We can be contacted at:
info@destiny.net.au

For assistance with your finance needs, contact:
finance@destiny.net.au

For download instructions, contact:
download@destiny.net.au

If you would like to tell us how you felt about this book or make a suggestion for future books, please contact:
margaret.lomas@destiny.net.au

 **Destiny**®Financial Solutions

PO Box 5400
Chittaway Bay NSW 2261
Ph: 1800 648 640
www.destiny.net.au

'Destiny' and 'DestinyTrack' are registered trademarks of Destiny Business Solutions P/L and are used by permission. All rights reserved.

From the Author

After I wrote *How to Make Your Money Last as Long as You Do*, people wrote to me, excited about the new opportunities they had discovered from the book. Where possible, I tried to email these people with answers to their numerous questions.

It was not long before I began to want to give people much more information than the first book allowed—the more mail I received the more I realised that so little is really known about property investing, even by the so-called experts.

Writing a book such as this one is easy for me, because I am so passionate about the topic. With such a wonderful opportunity at our feet, I marvel that people are not stampeding real estate offices demanding positive cash flow property!

I would never presume to give advice to people which I was not prepared to take myself. Every single word in this book is a result of personal experience, which has given rise to my own quest for information. Prior to writing my first book, I read dozens of books myself, becoming more frustrated at how difficult people could make a concept seem, and at how wrong many assumptions appeared to be.

I love to write almost as much as I enjoy seeing people achieve to the best of their ability. I have enjoyed nothing more than seeing readers become excited about their future and gain a confidence in their own abilities.

For my part I continue to practice what I preach, and I continue to live a frantic life. Each new day brings a new idea, and I thank God each day for my wonderfully inspirational husband and five supportive children, without whom I could never do the things which make my life so much fun.

I hope that you too can find this enthusiasm not only for life, but for a future which will be filled with profit and success!

Acknowledgments

No writer can achieve anything without an abundance of support from others. My books would not be possible without the help and support of the following people, to whom I would like to give my sincere thanks:

The staff in the Destiny Financial Solutions head office—for keeping the show on the road whenever I lock myself away to write, and for the professional and caring way they deal with all enquiries. Your commitment to me and all of my special clients is appreciated more than you can know.

The managers of our branches—I choose these people, not for their knowledge and experience (which they can acquire on the way) but for their genuine desire to help others. I am blessed to have such an empathic group of people who continually go that extra mile for all of our clients.

My wonderful family—my relatives enthusiastically read my manuscripts, my children put up with me when I am writing, and they all encourage me. Life would have no meaning without my family.

To Michael Teys—great friend and colleague, without whom much of my knowledge would never have been acquired – your expectations of me help me to strive to achieve.

And of course, Reuben—a husband like no other. This man chose to become a member of a ready-made family, and has risen to the task in a way which defies words. Most men would be threatened by a person such as me, but he is my biggest fan, my confidante and the one who inspires and encourages me most of all. Without Reuben there would be no book (and definitely no software as he is the genius behind this), so we are indebted to him. My passion for my writing and my work is only surpassed by my love for Reuben.

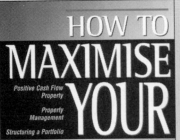